Daniel's Fight and Ours

Thomas D. Logie

Order this book online at www.trafford.com
or email orders@trafford.com

Most Trafford titles are also available at major online book retailers.

Printed in the United States of America.

ISBN: 978-1-4669-1897-9 (sc)
ISBN: 978-1-4669-1898-6 (e)

Trafford rev. 03/09/2012

 www.trafford.com

North America & International
toll-free: 1 888 232 4444 (USA & Canada)
phone: 250 383 6864 ♦ fax: 812 355 4082

CONTENTS

INTRODUCTION

We know neither the day nor the hour when the Lord Jesus will return, but only that His return is certain. For example, in two parables the ruler (a counterpart to either God the Father in the first instance in Matthew or the Lord Jesus Christ Himself in the second, soon to be returning to heaven—in Luke the order is reversed) left his homeland for a long interval. Matthew 21:33-45, 25:14-30; Mark 12:1-11; Luke 19:12-27, 20:9-18. In the one parable God left Israel tending His vineyard, and the people refused to pay rent (for example, the tithes as Haggai and Malachi warned) either literally or figuratively by way of true worship and obedience. In the second case two stewards were faithful to the Lord Jesus and one was lazy and as a consequence ended in the Lake of Fire and outer darkness. But one common element is the return of the Lord and final judgment, although the parable concerning Israel can also apply to the coming destruction of Jerusalem which was completed about 40 years later in 70 AD. One of the reasons for this book is the apparent nearness of our Lord's return in terms of human conditions mirroring previous epochs of judgment, either localized or worldwide. In Noah's time *the earth was filled with violence.* Genesis 6:11. Genesis 6:5 informs us that human imagination was shot through with evil. Do modern conditions, adjusting for vastly different technologies, mirror those of Noah's time? I believe so—you judge for yourself.

Genesis 11 records the Tower of Babel. Does humanity today look for a leader to help us get along without submitting to God? I would say so. I cannot think of a single country where Christians are respected for their Christianity, unless perhaps in South Korea and parts of the

United States and Nigeria. To me, the world looks like it is lurching toward one-man rule without fully perceiving the trap that Satan is setting for it. Again, you judge.

Is the rise of same-sex relationships an accident? The dispute is sharp in the United States, but the issue has arisen all over the world, including Israel. When Sodom and Gomorrah embraced these practices, what happened? Fire and brimstone fell from heaven, devastating the region to this very day. Genesis 18:20-19:30 tells the story. If one form of insanity can be defined as doing the same thing and expecting different results, then we see this form spreading rapidly through the whole world. But when viewing signs of immorality as a warning, we must remember for ourselves that it is only the grace of God that keeps us from the same or similar practices.

When Israel was judged, three of the most prevalent sins were greed, adultery and idolatry. A survey of any of the prophets will yield this conclusion. Amos and Hosea are two examples where these are prominent. Intoxication also appears in Amos 6. Once again, judge for yourselves whether these are prominent in the modern world.

The Lord Jesus said that *"the Gospel would be preached in all the world for a witness to all nations, and then the end shall come."* Matthew 24:13. This has largely occurred, although there may be a few isolated peoples who do not yet have the Bible and the Gospel in their languages. Missionaries are closing any remaining gaps.

Daniel 12:3 informs us that travel and knowledge will increase greatly shortly before the Last Judgment. That certainly is happening.

Lying to oneself and to others is also a salient sin of the last days. Already we can see across cultures an avoidance of the Holy Spirit, Who is called the Spirit of Truth in John 15:26. This is reflected in the avoidance of the Holy Bible, the written Word of Truth. It is also reflected in the denigration of the names of God and of Jesus, Who is the living Truth (John 14:6). Note the accusation of Romans 1:23 (and indeed Romans 1:16 through the rest of chapter 1) that humanity has suppressed the truth of conscience and has in its place worshiped idols of various sorts, including the worship of oneself or of a dictator. Since 1933 billions have worshiped the Fuehrer (Hitler), the Great Leader (Stalin), the Great Helmsman (Mao) and the succession of dictators in North Korea, to take several examples. Romans 1:24 teaches that God punishes those who worship false gods by removing the barriers to degrading sins. 2 Thessalonians 2:10-12 again stresses the importance of absolute truth and its absence in the context of the last days. If there is no worship in truth of God and of His Son (the Truth in human flesh) and of the Spirit of Truth, there is only everlasting doom for the individual.

In our times we face faster frauds than in any time of human history. The Internet can be a treasure trove of information, but it also enables thieves and liars to steal more money faster than at any time in the past. It likewise spreads slander faster than any printing press, with less chance for a defense by the target of the slander. Financial lies can be told and spread by "cooked books" as well as by words. Enron is but one example. These lies are but precursors of the lies to come that our Lord Jesus predicted in Matthew 24:23-24. Because humanity does not love the truth of Jesus Christ, God will as a preliminary part of His curse and judgment send "strong delusion" so that these devilish liars of the future will succeed in deceiving most of the human race to worship the Anti-Christ to its everlasting destruction. 2 Thessalonians 2:11. For now, I leave you to judge whether or not we are becoming a more truthful or less truthful society in assessing the figurative sign of the fig tree.

Revelation 9:21 lists four sins to which humanity clings even through the Great Tribulation: murders, sorceries (Greek *pharmakos*, indicating drug-induced origin), fornication (I understand this as a general terms that includes all form of sexual sin outside of monogamy) and thefts. Are the foundations for world-wide sins of these sorts already well laid? Once more, I leave the judgment to you.

Because I think that the woodpile is about ready and dry and that only the kindling and the lighter are not yet visible, I suspect that world-wide judgment may arrive before my normal life span would be completed, although I do not know this. We must remember that God has the power to speed up, slow down or even stop time, as He did for Joshua and Israel in Joshua 10:12-13. As a sign He even reversed time for King Hezekiah as recorded in 2 Kings 20:9-11. So we must be prepared either to life a normal life span (if God permits) or to face the full fury of humanity whipped up by Satan as part of his futile struggle to overthrow God as the Sovereign Lord over all Creation. Therefore I believe it prudent to dust off Old Testament prophecy written just before and during the judgments of Israel and Judah as miniature analogies to that struggle and to the Last Judgment to come. Daniel wrote concerning the judgment and lived through the Exile himself. Zephaniah and then Habakkuk wrote shortly before the judgment. I hope and pray that the reader will reflect on the similarities between the times of these prophets and our own times, even though our technologies are far more advanced as predicted by Daniel himself.

CHAPTER 1 —
THE PREVIOUS HUNDRED YEARS
IN A NUTSHELL

To have some understanding of the world into which Daniel was born, one should take a brief overview of the history of Judah from King Hezekiah forward. This starts over a century before Daniel's birth. As the Scriptures record in 2 Kings 17, the Assyrian Empire had finished off the Northern Kingdom and exiled its people, sending other captive peoples into the void created by the deportation of the Northern Kingdom survivors. We believe this event occurred in 722 or 721 BC. Hezekiah was in the 6th year of his reign when the Northern Kingdom fell (2 Kings 18:10).

One might reasonably have expected the Assyrians to keep on coming and attack Judah after having finished off the Northern Kingdom, but in the providence of God this did not happen. The Assyrians may have chosen to consolidate their grip on the territories already taken. They may also have been concerned about restiveness in the eastern end of their empire, an area from which Babylonia was to arise. In the 14th year of Hezekiah's reign, he suffered a severe setback when Assyria raided his kingdom, but this was abated by monetary payment (2 Kings 18:13-16). But Hezekiah was granted another respite before he was to face the full fury of Assyria in the 26th or 27th year of his 29-year reign, about 701 B.C. (recorded starting at 2 Kings 18:17 and 2 Chronicles 32). Isaiah was the most prominent prophet of the time, living in Jerusalem. He and King Hezekiah had an excellent relationship, reflected in Isaiah 36-39, especially Isaiah 38.

During the respite, King Hezekiah expanded northward into the territories of the destroyed Northern Kingdom, as reflected in the wonderful Passover service that Hezekiah celebrated as recorded in 2 Chronicles 30 when Hezekiah was able to send royal letters into former Northern Kingdom territory. This incorporated fragments of the Lost Tribes into Judah, but at the same time it would have come to the attention of the Assyrian authorities sooner or later. At this point Assyria was making a serious bid to be a Middle Eastern superpower. So when Assyria turned on King Hezekiah and on Judah about 701 B.C., complete conquest rather than financial gain was the objective. King Hezekiah had prepared numerous fortresses and had ordered the construction of the famous water tunnel which preserved Jerusalem's water supply and denied the same to anyone besieging Jerusalem. Hezekiah also had diplomatic connections to Assyria's enemies in the small but rising state of Babylon. But even with all this, by military weight Assyria should have prevailed. But the Assyrians vaunted themselves not only against Judah but against God Himself, and God intervened with the deadly plague that wiped out the army of Assyria (2 Chronicles 32:21, 2 Kings 19:35, Isaiah 37:36 document the slaughter of the Assyrian army. Isaiah 36-39 is the prophet's account of the entire campaign; 2 Kings 18-19 and 2 Chronicles 29-32 give an overview of Hezekiah's reign. Thereafter Assyria was embroiled with Babylon in steady warfare and had no further time to occupy Judah, which was too small to be more than an irritant.

But the keystone of Hezekiah's life and defense of Judah and Jerusalem was not military or engineering skill (although he had both) but faith in God Himself.

When Hezekiah died, his son King Manasseh took the throne, but it is hard to imagine a more unlike pair of father and son. (See 2 Kings 21 and 2 Chronicles 33 for fuller details.) For most of his long reign, Manasseh was subservient to the dominant power Assyria not only in paying tribute (which Hezekiah had done at least once) but also in establishing the Assyrian religion in Jerusalem and the Temple precincts. Manasseh sacrificed children (2 Chronicles 33:6) and was an ancient brutal dictator much like Saddam Hussein or Qaddafi of Libya in contemporary times (2 Kings 21:16). One prominent example was the brutal execution of Isaiah, his father's friend and God's prophet. King Manasseh had Isaiah sawed in half as a bloody warning that he would tolerate no prophet speaking in the name of the God of Israel (Hebrews 11:37, drawing on ancient Jewish testimony). Judah under Manasseh deteriorated to the point where God was determined to bring the judgment of conquest and exile (2 Kings 21:11-16), although the blows did not fall immediately.

Manasseh's total reign was 55 years. In 2 Chronicles 33:11-13, one finds one of the most remarkable genuine jailhouse conversions ever. King Manasseh had been taken by the Assyrians as a captive to Babylon and thrown in jail as an older man. As recorded in the remainder of 2 Chronicles 33, the change was real, but one can perceive that it came far too late to make any impression on Amon, Manasseh's son and immediate successor. Manasseh was not able to undo all the evil he had done earlier in his reign, as the preaching of Jeremiah would prove. His own guard killed Amon as Nero's guards were later to pressure Nero into committing suicide. This left Josiah as king, being but 8 years old. It was Josiah who was king when Daniel was born.

Unlike his father Amon, Josiah began to learn during the last, late, repentant phase of his grandfather Manasseh's life. Spiritually, Josiah resembled Hezekiah, the last great king of Judah before him. Josiah may not have known immediately of his grandfather's imprisonment by the Assyrians and certainly would have be horrified about this when he did find out. In any event, Manassah had done an about-face as to religion and died as a genuine worshiper of the God of Israel. Josiah was probably too young to remember the Assyrian idolatries that had existed in most of his grandfather's reign. Like Hezekiah, Josiah was a stout defender of the independence of Judah and a devout worshiper of the God of Israel. As a small nation having to deal with three larger neighbors (Assyria, Babylon, and Egypt), Judah had to have maintain a strong defense and also keep good diplomatic ties with the enemies of its main enemy, which at the beginning of King Josiah's reign was still Assyria. (Isaiah's prophecy [39:6] that Babylon would take Israel's treasure did not yet appear immediately likely of fulfillment, although that day came much faster than observers would have suspected. Will this pattern too be repeated in our world?)

Judah appeared to prosper as long as King Josiah reigned, although Jeremiah warned of the national spiritual rot underneath Josiah's genuine reverence. Even with godly Josiah on the throne, judgment was not far behind. The "lion in the thicket" of Jeremiah 4:7 is probably Babylon; in Daniel's vision King Nebuchadnezzar's Babylon was represented as a lion (Daniel 7:4). If one surveys Jeremiah 2-5, one finds a two-fold indictment: spiritual adultery in the form of worshiping other gods and thereby violating God's covenants with Israel (especially Moses and David), and physical adultery in violating the covenant between man and wife. Both of these reflect stubbornness of spirit and hardness of heart, the same reason our Lord Jesus gave in Matthew 19:8 for Moses' permission of divorce. So there was a veneer of righteousness atop a nation seething in sin. The story of King Josiah's heroic exertions to bring Judah back to God is told in 2 Kings 22 and 2 Kings 23:1-28 and also 2 Chronicles 34 and 2 Chronicles 35:1-19. In this volatile time of partial revival and conflict Daniel was born.

QUESTIONS FOR REFLECTION AND DISCUSSION:

1. If Hezekiah and Manasseh influenced their nation, you surely influence your family. To what extent is leaders' influence and our example for good or for evil?
2. Do we have the faith of Hezekiah to stand up for the name of God against overwhelming human force and power? Do we really believe that God can deliver?

3. God permitted Pharaoh to kill King Josiah in his human prime so that Josiah would not have the misery of seeing the downfall of Israel on earth. (Isaiah 57:1-2) If a believer seems to die a premature death, can we in the midst of grief accept this as the good will of God?

4. Some people by strict self-discipline can give the impression of keeping the outward parts of God's Law. This is well and good as far as it goes, but do we really delight inwardly in keeping God's law (Romans 7:22) like Hezekiah and Josiah or do we find it a constant strain even in our souls? How do we focus on both the battle to put to death our remaining sinful impulses (Romans 8:13) and the rest of faith that God gives (Hebrews 4:9-11)? Do we really delight in keeping God's commandments, even though our obedience is imperfect?

If we lift our focus beyond Israel to the Near East as a whole, an ancient pattern was about to break up, although few knew it. The classic pattern was for Egypt to be one major power in the Nile River valley and then there would be another Mesopotamian power on the upper or lower Tigris and Euphrates Rivers (Mari, Assyria or Hammurabi's Babylonia for example). Genesis 14 is an early example of a raid from a Mesopotamian coalition that temporarily captured Lot. The major powers would meet somewhere in what became Israel or Syria. Then the Hittites began to gain power in modern Turkey and come from the northwest, and the Sea People invaded Egypt from Cyprus or Crete and also established the Philistine cities. Moses had begun to break this pattern: after Pharaoh lost his army chasing Israel, Egypt never again secured lasting control of the Holy Land. But Egypt still raided as in the time of Rehoboam and Shishak (1 Kings 14:25-26). By the time Daniel was born, Assyria had come close to absolute power in the region but was slipping. Egypt wanted spoils for herself but also feared the rising power of Babylon. Judah traditionally was friendly with Babylon because of their common enemy Assyria. As Isaiah and later

Habakkuk, Zephaniah and Jeremiah prophesied, this balance of power system was about to collapse, and Judah with it. However, this was not predominantly a question of diplomacy or military strategy but rather was a direct result of the intervention of God to bring judgment upon adulterous Judah (for example, see Ezekiel 21). But the crash had not yet come when Daniel was born.

We have already mentioned Jeremiah's preaching. Habakkuk probably was also preaching during the last part of Jeremiah's ministry. While the book does not date itself, I have a clue from an Iranian immigrant who was once a client. He told me that Habakkuk's and Daniel's graves remain known in Iran to this day. With Daniel this would be obvious since his last written prophecy was in the third year of Cyrus, the great Persian ruler after the fall of Babylon (see Isaiah 45 for a prediction of his benevolent reign). But crediting my client's testimony would mean that Habakkuk survived the conquest of Judah and the long march to Babylon. He lived to see his prophecy fulfilled. Habakkuk was already an adult before Daniel was taken captive, since his prophetic warning was delivered while still in Judah. I have no basis to state how many years before the various battles Habakkuk spoke, but he must have at least old enough to be Daniel's father.

Zephaniah also preached during Josiah's reign, but we do not otherwise know whether his message was heard in the last part of that reign when Daniel would have been a young child. Because the destruction of Nineveh was still future (Zephaniah 2:13), one would infer that Zephaniah's preaching started earlier in Josiah's reign; we thus cannot know whether Daniel heard Zephaniah personally or not. It is possible that Zephaniah was already dead before Daniel was born. If this should be true, Daniel may or may not have been taught Zephaniah's prophecy while he still was in Jerusalem.

CHAPTER 2 —
ZEPHANIAH AS A BACKDROP OF DANIEL'S EARLY DAYS

As an introduction of Daniel and his times, we should look at Zephaniah for at least two reasons: (1) It is short enough not to drown Daniel as a primary subject; and (2) It is close enough historically that it a logical introduction to the turmoil in which Daniel grew up. One could equally study Jeremiah and Ezekiel, but they deserve their own separate studies. For our own instruction there is yet a deeper reason. The beginning of Zephaniah sounds a warning of total destruction like that of Revelation. The end of Zephaniah sounds a note of joy like the last two chapters of Revelation. So Zephaniah in focusing on Judah—the ostensible people of God of his day—was giving a message analogous to the warnings to His people of the Lord Jesus in Matthew 24 and in Revelation, and also the promises that He gave notwithstanding the terrible times of judgment to come. The destruction of Judah prophesied by Zephaniah and witnessed by Daniel and the destruction of Israel prophesied by Jesus Christ are both scaled-down models for the destruction of all civilizations in Revelation. In studying Zephaniah first and then comparing Habakkuk, which was probably written a bit later than Zephaniah but still before the Exile (and adding some extracts from Jeremiah and Ezekiel for additional detail) and then the book of Daniel and his life, we will have a miniaturized view of the end of days which will enable us to grasp better the tremendous changes to come.

Zephaniah first introduces himself and then with no effort to comfort his audience abruptly begins his message of doom:

I will utterly consume all from off the land, saith the LORD.
I will consume man and beast; I will consume the fowls of the heaven,
and the fishes of the sea [compare Revelation 8:8 and then 16:3], and
the stumblingblocks with the wicked; and I will cut off man from off
the land, saith the LORD.
I will also stretch out mine hand upon Judah, and upon all the
inhabitants of Jerusalem; and I will cut off the remnant of Baal from
this place, and the name of the Chemarims with the priests;
And them that worship the host of heaven upon the housetops; and
them that worship and that swear by the LORD, and that swear by
Malcham; [for comparison, read Ezekiel 8]
And them that are turned back from the LORD; and that have not
sought the LORD, nor enquired for him.
Hold thy peace at the presence of the Lord GOD: for the day of the
LORD [is] at hand: for the LORD hath prepared a sacrifice, He has
invited His guests. [compare Revelation 19:17-21]

QUESTION FOR REFLECTION AND DISCUSSION:

How would you react if your pastor started his sermon this way? How would your church react?

Do you think that this note of doom can be an appropriate way to start a sermon or a class? I realize that many hearers may be angry or even walk out rather than listen, but how do we digest the fact that the Holy Spirit led Zephaniah to say this at the start of his message? How does this compare to Jonah, who gave Nineveh 40 days before destruction (Jonah 3:4)? How can we expect people to repent if they are not told why they need to repent?

Much of the remainder of chapter 1 tells us that wealth (1:18), social standing or bloodlines will avail nothing against the coming judgment of God. In 1:8, Zephaniah tells us that the king's children and the princes will be punished notwithstanding their descent from King David. Perhaps Zephaniah could escape imprisonment for such shocking speech because he himself was descended from King Hezekiah, a worthy successor and descendent of David. (A little later Jeremiah was in fact imprisoned for his warnings. See Jeremiah 37:13-16). I do not know what to make of the "strange clothing" of Zephaniah 1:8. One possibility is that the royal family had the privilege of special clothing denied to the general population. Another is that members of the royal court wore the latest foreign fashions in somewhat the same way that people today seek the most chic styles. Still another possibility is that some people were cross-dressing (in violation of Deuteronomy 22:5) and Zephaniah was giving them special warning of the judgment to come. Perhaps the "strange clothing" was simply expensive and refined clothing beyond the means of most people. This understanding would be in line with the special warnings that riches will do no good. Perhaps various types of people were all intended targets of the warning.

Similarly, there are various views about "leaping on the threshold", ranging from idol-worship to burglary. While we cannot at this distance in time and culture be exactly sure of the specific targets of specific warnings in Zephaniah, we can readily see that to some extent the entire nation was being warned. The exiles included all sorts and types of people, from faithful Daniel to the wicked King Zedekiah, who has his eyes gouged out just after he saw his sons slaughtered because of his rebellion against King Nebuchadnezzar of Babylon against Jeremiah's warnings (2 Kings 25:7).

A prevailing attitude in Zephaniah's day which has reappeared in our own times is that *the Lord will not do good, neither will He do evil (v.12)*." During the times of the founding of the United States, this was a fashionable intellectual belief called deism, but it was definitely a minority view and remained so for at least the next 150 years. The idea was that God wound up the clock of nature and then turned His back and let it run without further interference. On the continent of Europe, many people deny the very existence of God, as do most evolutionists in the United States. This attitude undermines the healthy fear of God because it undercuts the idea that He will uphold the right and destroy the wrong. The concept of an indifferent God and the idea of God's judgment cannot co-exist.

Those who argue for a God Who intervenes on behalf of His chosen people are ridiculed at most prominent universities today except those with express religious ties. But the evidence is overwhelming in favor of a God Who intervenes on behalf of truth. The Jewish people survived from about 605 B.C. until 1948 with practically no military and no national state of any significance. Hebrew was virtually dormant as a spoken language. This is unparalleled. The Christian Church has survived persecution for nearly 2000 years with no established military and no fixed territory in which to reside. At times Christians have exercised political influence, but it has been rare for born-again Christians to hold office for consecutive and extended periods of time. Queen Victoria of England may be a rare example, but she did not have the full power of government at any time. Benjamin Disraeli and William Gladstone both professed Christianity during Queen Victoria's long reign, as did Lord Salisbury near the end of her reign. In turn, his nephew Arthur Balfour committed Great Britain to a Jewish homeland in what was then called Palestine in 1917, which grew into the modern nation of Israel over about 30 years. Since the principles of political power and military force do not explain the survival of the people of Israel nor of Biblical Christianity, one must look elsewhere for an explanation. That explanation is the protection of God from the full measure of human hatred for the people of God. For example, consider the Lord's words to Ezekiel in Ezekiel 11:16-17:

> *Therefore say, "Thus says the Lord, Although I have cast them far off among the heathen and although I have scattered them among the countries, yet I will be to them as a little sanctuary in the countries where they shall come."*

Therefore say, "Thus says the Lord, I will even gather you out of the people and assemble you out of the countries where you have been scattered, and I will give you the land of Israel."

Despite the frequent lack of faith on the part of the people of Israel, this prophecy has held good from roughly 600 BC when Ezekiel first said and wrote it through today, because God Almighty has so ordered. He is preparing for the time when He will bring to both the world and the true Church *"life from the dead"* (Romans 11:15) from Israel. God's purposes will come true!

Starting with George Washington, there has been a strong understanding in the United States military of the providential intervention of God in military affairs and in affairs of state. George Washington and George Patton were very different men, but both shared a deep conviction that God had a destiny for them that He would make sure that they fulfilled before they died. Douglas MacArthur agreed. Abraham Lincoln was especially outspoken in his belief that God providentially controlled the Civil War in a manner that neither North nor South intended or anticipated. Many historians classify Thomas Jefferson as a deist for some period in his life. But if he retained those convictions, how could Thomas Jefferson say that "I tremble for my nation when I remember that God is just"? And how could Jefferson have written in the Declaration of Independence that that the Creator "has endowed [people] with certain inalienable rights, among which are life, liberty and the pursuit of happiness"? I will agree as a matter of history that during much of his life Jefferson did not believe in miracles nor in the deity of Jesus Christ, but not even Jefferson believed that God ignored human conduct. He did not agree with the intellectuals of Zephaniah's day nor with our modern intellectuals that God can or should be ignored because He ignores our thoughts and actions, assuming that He exists at all. To the contrary, we shall be judged by our words (Matthew 12:36-37), our actions (Revelation 20:12) and even our thoughts (Psalm 139:2-4 and indeed the entire Psalm).

It would be too large a diversion to tackle the entire subject of fulfilled prophecy, but it should be sufficient for basic purposes to realize the detail of the prophecies fulfilled in the death, burial and resurrection of our Lord Jesus Christ. As an introductory sampler, I would point the reader to 2 Samuel 7, Isaiah 7, 9, 40 and 42; to Job 19:23-27; to Psalms 16, 22 and 69; to Micah 5:2 and to Isaiah 53. At least one scholar has counted 300 prophecies fulfilled by Jesus Christ. For the moment, I am using the fulfillments directed by God as but one extended series of constant divine interventions in human history. Certainly the entire book of Esther is another. We do not worship a passive God or one Who is frustrated, but a God Who is patiently and sovereignly working His will against both demonic and human opposition to bring to pass His divine purposes at their appointed times. The critics of Zephaniah's day and their modern counterparts are not just wrong but egregiously wrong.

Abraham Lincoln in the later part of his life had pronounced views concerning the question of whether God is indifferent to human affairs. His views as a younger man may have been different, but as a mature man Lincoln knew that he needed God's help. I offer several quotes as representative of his most mature thinking and also as a fair representation of the traditional American view as to whether God is indifferent as Zephaniah's contemporaries thought. With regard to the Bible itself, Wikipedia quotes Lincoln as saying this:

> *In regards to this great Book (the Bible), I have but to say it is the best gift God has given to man. All the good the Savior gave to the world was communicated through this Book. But for it we could not know right from wrong. All things most desirable for man's welfare, here and hereafter, are found portrayed in it.*

Clearly, if God has given the Bible He has intervened in history and cares very much for us. But Lincoln during the Civil War was far more explicit. For example, consider these quotes (with emphasis added) from the Gettysburg Address and then from the Second Inaugural Address:

> *Fourscore and seven years ago our fathers brought forth upon this continent a new nation, conceived in liberty, and dedicated to the proposition that all men are created equal. We here highly resolve that the dead shall not have died in vain, that this nation,* **under God***, shall have a new birth of freedom and that government of the people, by the people, and for the people, shall not perish from the earth.*

> *Neither [North nor South] anticipated that the cause of the conflict slavery might cease with, or even before, the conflict itself should cease. Each looked for an easier triumph, and a result less fundamental and astounding. Both read the same Bible, and pray to the same God and each invokes His aid against the other. It may seem strange that any men should dare to ask a just God's assistance in wringing their bread from the sweat of other men's faces but let us judge not that we be not judged. The prayers of both could not be answered; that of neither has been answered fully . . .*

> *With malice toward none with charity for all with firmness in the right,* **as God gives us to see the right***, let us strive on to finish the work we are in.*

Even more strongly, Lincoln said this:

> "**Woe unto the world because of offenses!** *for it must needs be that offenses come; but woe to that man by whom the offense cometh." If we shall suppose that American slavery is one of those offenses which, in the providence of God, must needs come, but which, having continued through his appointed time, he now wills to remove, and that he gives to both North and South this terrible war, as the woe due to those by whom the offense came, shall we discern therein any departure from those divine attributes which the believers in a living God always ascribe to him? Fondly do we hope—fervently do we pray—that this mighty scourge of war may speedily pass away. Yet, if God wills that it continue until all the wealth piled by the bondman's two hundred and*

*fifty years of unrequited toil shall be sunk, and until every drop of blood drawn with the lash shall be paid by another drawn with the sword, as was said three thousand years ago, so still it must be said, "**The judgments of the Lord are true and righteous altogether**."*

These quotations are not unique but represent Lincoln's thought. Examples of shorter Lincoln quotes follow, showing how dependent on God's intervention Lincoln truly was.

The Almighty has His own purposes.

I can see how a man can look down upon the earth and be an atheist, but I cannot conceive how he could look up into the heavens and say there is no God.

I have been driven to my knees many times because there was no place else to go.

I know that the Lord is always on the side of the right. But it is my constant anxiety and prayer that I and this nation should be on the Lord's side.

Let us have faith that right makes might, and in that faith let us dare to do our duty as we understand it.

From the standpoint of accurate American history, to think of Abraham Lincoln as President without knowing of his faith in Jesus Christ is inconceivable. Whether you agree with his faith or not, it is a historical fact. I do not exaggerate in saying that without the faith of Abraham Lincoln in his Savior two nations instead of one would have emerged from the Civil War for the simple reason that Lincoln could not have functioned as President without his faith. But more than American history is at stake in the intellectual struggle pinpointed by Zephaniah. The issue is whether human history is simply what men and women make it or whether it is being directed by God to an end of which He has warned us through the prophets such as Zephaniah, Habakkuk and Daniel (and most of all, by Jesus Christ Himself).

Abraham Lincoln made no bones about his opinion: *The Almighty has His own purposes.*

Abraham Lincoln, like all of us, was fallible. But his view of the intervention of God was in accord with the Holy Scriptures. We have already been reminded of Noah's Flood and of how God turned Sodom and Gomorrah into scorched earth, some possibly under water, which has not recovered since. Other instances of the direct intervention of God are found in Genesis 37:7-10, in Numbers 16:29-33 and in Acts 12:23. The history of Job is another extended example. For now, it is sufficient to establish that the Bible teaches that God controls human events and from time to time intervenes forcefully to carry out His own plans.

As Zephaniah 1:13 and the following verses show, God would prove his intervention to Zephaniah's generation by destroying them and their property and dragging the survivors as prisoners to Babylon. Then as now, many wealthy people thought that they could buy their way out of trouble. Not so. God's judgment fell on rich and poor alike, as it will fall indiscriminately during the Last Days (Revelation 19:18). As the adults of Moses' generation were barred from the Promised Land for their unbelief, so Zephaniah's listeners would be expelled from the Promised Land for their unbelief. With the 70-year exile, practically none of the exiles returned, though some of their descendants did. Fundamentally, the intellectuals of Zephaniah's time were like most intellectuals in the Western world today in denying God's control. Today, even God's existence is denied by the prevailing intellectual leaders of most secular universities. Peter perceived a similar attitude in 2 Peter 3:3-13 with respect to Noah's Flood. Today it is fashionable to laugh about both the Flood and the fire and brimstone that struck Sodom and Gomorrah. God's judgment fell on Zephaniah's generation, and God has not changed His character one bit. I cannot predict with any precision when God's judgment will fall nor whether any particular person will be alive when it strikes, and I cannot exclude a temporary reprieve like that of the time of Jonah for Nineveh if we see real repentance and spiritual change. But Nineveh's reprieve ran out, and sooner or later the time of this earth will run out too.

QUESTION FOR REFLECTION AND DISCUSSION:

1. Do we think, feel and live as if the judgment of God is a certainty? Do we really believe it?
2. How do we compare the character of God from Zephaniah's time to now? In considering this, look at Malachi 3:6, James 1:17 and Hebrews 13:8 and other passages that you find.

Zephaniah 2 predicts the destruction of both Judah and of the surrounding peoples and of Ethiopia also. Since Nineveh had not yet been destroyed as of this writing, we can confirm that Zephaniah wrote before Babylon's final attack against Assyria and its capital Nineveh had succeeded. King Josiah was still alive. So we have the appeal to the meek in Zephaniah 2:3, which I believe should be read as a double appeal. As an immediate appeal it should be read as addressed to the people of the land of Israel who heard or read Zephaniah's message. Yet it can also be read as an appeal to the meek anywhere on earth at any time, similar to Isaiah's invitation in Isaiah 1:18: *"Come now and let us reason together, says the Lord. Though your sins be as scarlet, they shall be white as snow. Though they be red like crimson, they shall be as wool."* Additional confirmation comes from the words of the Lord Jesus in the Beatitudes: *"Blessed are the meek, for they shall inherit the earth."* Matthew 5:5.

Those who know Hebrew well inform us that the Hebrew word for "land" and "earth" is the same. I believe that God intentionally chose to use Hebrew for nearly all of the Old Testament with full knowledge of the double meaning of the Hebrew word. In many cases it is legitimate to read the prophecies using this word with both meanings, as I suggest here. The prophecy of Isaiah 7:14 is a similar case with the use of a word that can mean both "woman" and "virgin." In fact one royal birth within a few years and a second royal Virgin Birth hundreds of years later were both within Isaiah's meaning. There is still a further double meaning of "breath" and "spirit" which is helpful to a fuller grasp of Ezekiel 36-39. In many such cases one should consider whether both possible meanings fit the Scriptures as a whole and the immediate context.

A further observation is to note the distinction between Judah on the one hand and Moab and Ammon on the other. Judah was promised restoration, but by reason of pride Moab and Ammon were condemned to perpetual desolation (Zephaniah 2:8-11). Judah was also promised the land of the Philistines, although the language there was not quite so forceful as with Moab and Ammon. One major lesson is that the sin of pride can be among the most offensive sins of all in God's sight—just as offensive as the scarlet sins of Sodom and Gomorrah. Indeed, King Nebuchadnezzar will be another example of pride, although in the end like King Manasseh he was humbled and forgiven. The proud will be destroyed forever from the presence of God in everlasting thirst and dryness, just as the proud Ammonites and Moabites were destroyed by the Babylonians and their physical land parched.

QUESTIONS FOR REFLECTION AND DISCUSSION:

1. How are we fighting pride in our lives? If we are seeking meekness and humility before God, does thanksgiving help?
2. Did Zephaniah's word concerning the lands of Moab and Ammon (roughly speaking, modern Jordan) come true? Are they mostly desert today? Are we aware of Ammonites and Moabites today? What is the prophetic significance of the fact that Bedouin Arabs—descendants of Abraham through Ishmael—adapted to desert conditions live there now?

I believe that Zephaniah 3 also has a double application to the coming exile in Daniel's time and to the end of the age, which is surely coming and may be around the corner. I suggest that the predominant theme is the end of days after verse 4. How shocking is the description of the leadership of Israel after the death of Josiah. Zephaniah 3:3 likens them to hyenas! Zephaniah 3:6-7 records that the Jewish people had not learned from the fearful destruction that various nations had suffered. This might refer to the wars between Babylon and Assyria that were then raging, but the modern setting is clearest with the destructiveness of two world wars, especially in Europe and Japan. Even without Biblical history, an observer should see how godless nations have suffered for their unbelief in God from 20th century history. The providences involved in the partial regathering of Israel that we now see should convince an honest observer that God was and remains at work. In fact Zephaniah 3:8-11 makes reference to the gathering and destruction of the nations (Revelation 16:16 and then 19:17-21) and to the regathering of the people and then their final turn to God, also mentioned in Romans 11:26-29. As to the destruction of the nations, a miniature we can grasp is how Jehu gathered the worshipers of Baal into a pavilion and then killed them (2 Kings 10:18-28). Concerning God's mercy, the word "dispersed" in Zechariah 3:10 is the counterpart to the modern diaspora. Indeed, we already know that some of the dispersed have returned to Israel from Ethiopia. One day all of Israel will return to their spiritual home with God the Father and His Son and Messiah, Jesus of Nazareth, to be joined with the faithful remnant from all nations. Then all the joyous verses of the last part of Zephaniah 3 will come true.

Focus on the scene of Zephaniah 3:17 in which the Lord sings to His people. He will sing a triumphant spiritual love song of a quality that has not been heard yet. Imagine the power and comfort of that voice like a waterfall (my understanding of Revelation 1:15)! Not even Beethoven's Ninth nor Handel's Messiah will come close to that. It will be an undeserved honor to be in the audience, to be part of that Bride to whom our Lord will sing, and to hear that tremendous voice that will dwarf Jerome Hines, Caruso and any other singer one may mention. I envision this as part of the marriage supper of the Lamb in Revelation 19:7-9. It is even possible that in heaven there will be a perpetual solo by the Messiah, our Lord Jesus, with a response from us as a multi-part choir.

Like Revelation, Zephaniah opens with judgment and destruction and closes with joy and triumph. So too Daniel's life would start with exile and disaster and end in wonderful fellowship with God and great authority in Persia.

QUESTION FOR REFLECTION AND DISCUSSION:

To what extent do you feel or sense the coming victory of Jesus Christ and the heavenly worship that will follow? When you get some sense of this, does this relieve your anxiety (consider Matthew 6:25-34 and Philippians 4:6)?

CHAPTER 3 —
A QUICK SURVEY OF HABAKKUK

Habakkuk was nearly contemporary with Zephaniah (probably a bit later) and with Jeremiah forms a bridge in time from Zephaniah to Daniel. So we will take a quick scan of Habakkuk, trusting that this will stimulate all of us to examine both Zephaniah and Habakkuk more carefully. I have been told by an Iranian refugee in the United States that the locations in modern Iran (ancient Persia) of the tombs of both Daniel and Habakkuk are known to this day.

Habakkuk does not identify the reigning king when he wrote. Given the substance of what the Holy Spirit said through Habakkuk, an educated guess would be that Habakkuk wrote after the death of King Josiah but before the first capture of Jerusalem by Nebuchadnezzar, which we date at approximately 605 BC. The Books of Kings and Chronicles show four weak kings during this time, all of whom were beholden either to Egypt or to Babylon. None was truly independent. This is the most logical reason why Habakkuk does not identify the king or kings in power. Not only did the kings change rapidly, but they were too weak to exercise the powers associated with kings. Judean kings had paid tribute to foreigners before, as did Hezekiah for a time and as had Manasseh for most of his reign. But this was worse—the foreign interference was constant and intrusive. Worse yet, Habakkuk was given the message that God was not finished in judging Judah. He would going to bring Babylon down on Judah like a ton of bricks!

Habakkuk knew that Judah was in a morally depraved condition. One measure is found in Habakkuk 1:2-4, where justice is perverted regularly. If one were to scan Jeremiah, a contemporary of Habakkuk who wrote far more extensively, one would find many more reasons why God brought judgment. For example, Jeremiah 2:11-13 points out that the people of Judah were worshiping other gods. How foolish! Not only had the nation as a whole abandon the true and living waters, like the sweet waters that God had provided at Elim during the Exodus, but they had in self-reliance had made cracked cisterns that could not hold water at all. So spiritually, they were dying of thirst and doing nothing constructive about it.

In Jeremiah 5 we find other dimensions to Judah's depravity. Verses 1-3 show that lying and even perjury were rampant. In part these verses parallel Habakkuk 1:2-4, but they seem to go even further. Consider carefully the second portion of Jeremiah 5:1: *If you can find a man, if there be any that executes justice, that seeks the truth and I will pardon [Jerusalem].* This is even worse than Sodom. When Abraham interceded for Sodom on God's behalf, he was told by God that if one could find 10 righteous people in Sodom that God would withhold the judgment (Genesis 18:32). In truth there was but one—righteous Lot, whom God's angels brought out of Sodom with his family—and even Lot's wife looked back to her destruction. Yet God says through Jeremiah that the presence of one righteous person—like Lot, not even of Abraham's stature— would cause Him to spare Jerusalem the conquest that befell her. But not one was found in the Jerusalem of Habakkuk and Jeremiah (from a land transaction found in Jeremiah 32 it appears that Jeremiah was from Anathoth, north of Jerusalem).

Jeremiah 5:7-9 connects a sexual dimension to the false worship already mentioned in Jeremiah 2. The people of Jerusalem worshiped false gods that had never delivered them or their ancestors and in reflection of that spiritually adulterous worship (see Hosea 1-3 for an earlier exposition of this theme when both the Northern and Southern Kingdoms still existed) and in reflection of that false worship gave the prostitutes of Jerusalem a booming business. As a consequence God lowered the boom on Jerusalem in the person of Nebuchadnezzar, a military genius first Crown Prince and then King of Babylon.

Ezekiel 8 shows that the corrupted worship was not just among the city population but extended into the Temple itself. The same building complex that Solomon had dedicated to the worship of the true God was now the place of idolatry. So God gave over not only the city but the Temple to destruction. Ezekiel 10 and 11:22-24 record the departure of the Spirit from the Temple (most specifically, from above the mercy seat in the Holy of Holies) to clear the way for the Babylonian destroyers.

Then Habakkuk has an honest question for God: I understand the evil of the people of Judah, but the Babylonians are even worse and even more violent. How can You use them and favor their military over Israel when they are even worse than us (paraphrasing and summarizing Habakkuk 1:6-17)?

An initial observation is that God did not criticize Habakkuk for asking such a question. In our prayers and meditations we should be honest with God. He already knows what we are thinking (Psalm 139:1-4). God instructed Habakkuk to write His answer in a way that anyone could read. In one respect it might be the ancient equivalent of a neon sign on a heavily traveled freeway. I would summarize several answers out of Habakkuk 2:

1. The most important thing to remember is "*The just shall live by faith.*" We will not see perfect justice in our current bodies and many people may not even live in a nation where anything resembles justice. But we must have faith that Jesus Christ will render justice at the end. Indeed this phrase from Habakkuk 2:4 is quoted by Paul the Apostle in Romans 1:17, and much of Romans 3 (especially Romans 3:6) is devoted to the necessity of the Last Judgment (described by the Lord Jesus in Matthew 25 and in many other places).

2. The Babylonians will have their turn of judgment also. Jeremiah 51 describes this in more detail. They will not get away with their sins.
3. Individual as well as national justice will be done.
4. The knowledge of the Lord will eventually extend beyond Israel to all nations.

Much of this tells of the judgment of God, in microcosm to come in Habakkuk's own days upon Judah. A devastating invasion is pictured. Some of the language is too broad to be confined to ancient Judah and in the light of Revelation must apply to the end of human history, which may be nearer than most of us think. As our Lord Jesus said, *"Now learn a parable of the fig tree. When it is tender and puts forth leaves, you know that summer is near. So when you see these things [spoken in Mark 13, Matthew 24 and Luke 21]know that it is near, at the doors."* Mark 13:28-29. Yet in Habakkuk 3:2 there is the counterpoint to the message of judgment: *"In wrath remember mercy."* Then starting in verse 17 there is one of the most famous praises in all of Scripture, which again echoes Job. Habakkuk said he would praise God even if all of his food supplies should fail. Job said, *"The Lord gave and the Lord has taken away; blessed be the name of the Lord."* Job 1:21. Our love for God should not depend on how or whether He protects our temporary riches or even our apparent necessities. Many Christians around the world suffer poverty and discrimination for their faith. Some are martyred, in which case their troubles are over and their everlasting joys have begun. Habakkuk closes in faith that God will strengthen and preserve him somehow, whatever may come.

QUESTIONS FOR REFLECTION AND DISCUSSION

1. How dependent is your happiness upon things of this world that will be swept away?

2. Which blessings do you value most: those you have now or those to come?
3. Can and will you praise God when life is hard or even full of despair?

CHAPTER 4 —
HISTORICAL SETTING FOR DANIEL

Jeremiah started his prophecy in the 13th year of Josiah's reign, which would have been 18 years before Josiah's death. This would mean that Jeremiah had been speaking for 21 or 22 years before Daniel was taken captive. It would be reasonable to imagine that Jeremiah was about 50 years older than Daniel, and the gap may well have been wider. But Daniel, having been precocious, probably heard as a young child something of both Jeremiah and Habakkuk and could possibly have known about Zephaniah also. Daniel would also have been aware of Jeremiah's advice to the early exiles in Jeremiah 29 after he arrived in Babylon. They would have to prepare for an extended exile. Much later, Daniel realized that the time of the exile was over from reading Jeremiah, the leading prophet of his young childhood (Daniel 9:2, referring to Jeremiah 25-11-12, 29:10).

So far as we can tell, Ezekiel prophesied to the exiles after the first deportations. He had been trained for the priesthood (based on inferences from Ezekiel's writings) but there is no indication that Ezekiel had yet reached the age of 30 when he would have started serving as a priest. Instead he was an adult prophet in exile while Daniel was in his school years and for a substantial time thereafter. Ezekiel was clearly familiar with Daniel as a young man (Ezekiel 14:14), so it is almost certain that Daniel likewise was familiar with Ezekiel.

From this it is reasonable to think that Jeremiah would have been of the generation of Daniel's grand-parents. Habakkuk would have been younger than Jeremiah but older than Ezekiel. Ezekiel was probably about the age of Daniel's parents, or perhaps slightly younger. So God placed His prophets in a position to influence Daniel indirectly in addition to implanting His Holy Spirit within Daniel (1 Peter 1:10-11 teaches that the Spirit lived within the prophets. As an aside, this explains David's prayer—David was also a prophet as well as a king—in Psalm 51:11 to God that He would not take His Holy Spirit from him.) Daniel would need all of this to resist the manifold temptations of the Babylonian court and its intrigue.

In several places I have stated that Daniel was a young child when he was taken captive. On what basis? First, he must have been castrated before puberty for castration to have served its intended purpose fully. Second, we have the consideration that Daniel lived at least into the third year of the reign of Cyrus of Persia (Daniel 10:1). Given the 70 years of the captivity that Daniel and all of Judah served to the first year of Darius (who was the interim ruler when Babylon fell—see Daniel 5:31), Daniel may well have been approximately 80 years old when Darius took over. If this is also the first year of Cyrus mentioned in Ezra 1:1, Daniel was about 80 years old when Cyrus permitted the Jewish people to return home. Otherwise Daniel would have been still older when Cyrus rendered his decree. We know that Daniel was so vigorous and able (Daniel 6:4) that Darius planned to place Daniel in charge of the entire administration. So I have to think that Daniel was at most 10 years old when he was taken into exile. If he were older, then he would have been in his mid-80s in Darius' time. Knowing what we know about modern elderly statesmen such as Gladstone, Churchill, Reagan and Adenauer, even an 80-year-old leader of such vigor and power is a stretch, although possible. It is highly improbable that Daniel was 85 or more and still able to work full days at intensive, demanding mental work. So projecting back I think it unlikely that Daniel was older than 10 and may have been as young as age 8 or so when he was captured.

The immediate chain of events that led to Daniel's captivity and castration began with a renewal of the long war for domination of the Middle East between a fading Assyrian Empire and a rising new Babylonian Empire under the leadership of Nebuchadnezzar's father, with Nebuchadnezzar as Crown Prince. Egypt feared Babylonia and therefore sought to prop up the Assyrian Empire, which Egypt no longer viewed as a serious threat to itself. This was a classic effort by Egypt to maintain a balance of power among potential enemies. To assist Assyria, Pharaoh wanted to send troops north and needed free passage through Judah. Pharaoh asked Josiah for this as recorded in 2 Chronicles 35:21. King Josiah had a grave decision to make.

The Egyptian request was an affront to the sovereignty of Judah, just as the German request for free passage through Belgium to reach France was an attack on Belgium's sovereignty at the start of World War 1. Moses hundreds of years earlier had asked for free passage through Edom near the end of the Exodus in order to enter the Promised Land and was rebuffed (Numbers 20:14-21). This refusal poisoned relations between Israel and Edom for centuries. So the Egyptian request was not totally without precedent. But could the Egyptians be trusted to keep their promise not to harm Judah during the passage? And how was the Egyptian Army to return to its homeland at the end of the fighting? Unlike Moses' request, the Egyptian Army would have to enter and pass through twice.

Further, Babylon had traditionally been Judah's friend and Assyria had been her mortal enemy since the days of Hezekiah. The Assyrian Empire had devastated much of Judah less than a century earlier and had jailed Manasseh, Josiah's grandfather. Assyria had exiled brutally the surviving inhabitants of the Northern Kingdom and also had been the source of the terrible idolatry of Manasseh, which idolatry Josiah had suppressed. Like the model for Dracula centuries later, the Assyrians had used public impalement as a means of killing those selected for public execution when they sacked a city. Why should Josiah offend a powerful and rising friend in order to assist an ancient foe that had caused all Israel so much harm? The Assyrians of Josiah's time were far from the repentant generation to whom Jonah had preached perhaps 2 centuries earlier. Beyond that, Nahum had prophesied the destruction of Nineveh, the traditional capital of Assyria. Was not now the time for that prophecy to be fulfilled?

In hindsight, we can see that advocates of politics based on balance of power would have argued that Josiah should have agreed to the Egyptian request to try to keep Babylon from becoming too strong. But King Josiah first and foremost was a man of faith in God, and to have stood by while Egypt combined with Assyria would have been a denial of his core faith and in particular Josiah's faith that God would defend his nation. So Josiah denied the request and barred the Egyptians' route at Megiddo—the same Armageddon where the world's armies will be assembled for the final slaughter at the word of Jesus Christ. Revelation 16:16. In the following battle King Josiah was killed and Egypt forced its way through, but too late to accomplish anything to help Assyria. On their return trip they temporarily turned Judah into an Egyptian puppet state.

In my judgment King Josiah faced a problem with no human solution. We cannot know whether or not the earlier presence of an Egyptian army would have made any significant difference in the Babylonian destruction of Assyria. Because of the deterioration of Assyrian morale by this time (see for example Nahum 2:10, 3:11-13), I don't think so. Probably the Babylonians would have shown less patience with Judah than they did in the actual case if King Josiah had assisted Egypt in its fight against Babylon. (See Jeremiah 39:11-14 and Jeremiah 39-40 generally for examples. Also, 2 Chronicles 36 and 2 Kings 23:25 to the end of 2 Kings give an overview of Babylonian administration over Judah.) Perhaps Daniel would not have been given the opportunities he actually received in Babylon if Josiah had been hostile to Babylon instead of his actual adherence to Judah's traditional alliance. Perhaps Ezekiel could not have taught openly in Babylon if Judah had behaved as an enemy when Josiah lived. Above all, we should note that God had sovereignly ordained the humanly tragic result for at least three purposes:

1) To judge Judah for its accumulated sins (2 Kings 22:16-17, 23:26-27);

2) To spare Josiah the misery of living through the time of judgment (2 Kings 22:18-20—see also Isaiah 57:1 and 2 Chronicles 34:24-27) and

3) To destroy the existing balance of power and open the way for the four great empires of Daniel's visions which in turn would be God's instruments (although very far from perfect—Babylon would even symbolize the harlot in Revelation, as a comparison of Isaiah 47 and Revelation 17 will show) to preserve the people of Israel and set the stage for the coming of Messiah, Jesus Christ of Nazareth.

The death of Josiah was the end of the functional independence of Judah and of the world of Daniel's young childhood. For a brief time Egypt re-established hegemony over the Holy Land, but Babylon would not tolerate this after Egypt's attempt to help Assyria, now crushed. After three years Egypt's chosen vassal had to switch allegiance to Babylon to avoid total destruction, but even this only postponed the agony. At this time Daniel, Ezekiel and probably Habakkuk were immediately exiled in Babylon, which Jeremiah was still in Jerusalem after the first deportation in which Daniel and Ezekiel were forced to go to Babylon. During the second and third attacks by Nebuchadnezzar upon Jerusalem Daniel was either in training or already in Babylonian government service. Given God's command through Jeremiah for the exiles to settle in and submit, Daniel did no wrong in serving the Babylonian government even if it were attacking the remainder of Daniel's own people because of their rebellion against Babylon (with the ultimate cause under the surface being the people's continuing rebellion against God Himself.)

Thomas D. Logie

QUESTIONS FOR REFLECTION AND DISCUSSION:

1. Does God still judge nations in modern times?
2. What happens to Christians within nations that may be under God's judgment? Does God protect them on earth? Does he sustain them to the extent they face hardship?
3. Would we have followed Jeremiah's advice to surrender to Babylon had we lived in those times? (Read Jeremiah 27, especially verse 12) How was this situation different from a demand that we submit to a world economic order that involves allegiance to 666 and to the Anti-Christ?

CHAPTER 5 —
Daniel in Training: A summary of Daniel 1

Even though Daniel came to the favorable notice of Nebuchadnezzar's talent scouts and was selected for immediate deportation to Babylon for that reason, there can be no question that he was a slave at the mercy of his captors, subject to God's overall sovereignty. While Nebuchadnezzar was highly unusual and ahead of his time in permitting responsibility and status to people of captive or enemy origin (as Alexander the Great and Napoleon were later to do), Nebuchadnezzar maintained absolute dictatorship through his loyal officials.

The first step in Daniel's exile would have been a difficult march of several hundred miles on foot through rough and sometimes desert country that would have been basically the reverse of Abraham's migration. This in itself was no easy task. Each day would have emphasized Daniel's physical helplessness in the face of his captors and would have separated him further from his parents and from his former home in Jerusalem. So far as we know, Daniel was never to see his parents again.

[The following subject matter may disturb some readers. In my judgment, this is not suitable for pre-teens. As on many occasions, the Bible tells the truth even when unpleasant.]

Kings in ancient times often maintained harems of women for their pleasure or at a minimum to fill out parties at the court. From such a king's standpoint, men were needed to supervise these women and attend to their maintenance and housing. Kings would not trust such women to ordinary men who are subject to sexual temptation. So ancient kings would castrate young men before puberty so that these castrated men could be in contact with the women without the king fearing that an affair would result. If this were done, the emasculated man would be virtually useless as a warrior or as a physical worker because he would be deprived of the muscle growth necessary to become competent at tasks requiring physical strength. However, he would be ideally suited for duty at the king's court. In a later era, China's most famous admiral was a eunuch. Princess Sultana encountered a eunuch in the 20th century in Saudi Arabia. In the days of King Nebuchadnezzar and for many centuries thereafter, captives had no human rights so far as human legal systems were concerned.

Daniel was one of those about whom our Lord Jesus spoke in Matthew 19:12: *there are some who have been made eunuchs by men . . . .* From the standpoint of the Mosaic law, Daniel could never worship in the Temple again. (Deuteronomy 23:1, see also Leviticus 21:17-24) God knew, although Daniel was probably too young to understand yet, that soon enough nobody would be worshiping at Solomon's Temple because it would be destroyed. Marriage and family were denied him for the rest of his life. He would never become robust physically. His only career could be in government service. A child of lesser faith may have feared that God had abandoned him by allowing such an atrocious act to be performed on him as if he were a horse instead of a man, but Daniel's faith proved to be strong even as a young child.

Having been deprived of his manhood and masculinity, Daniel entered the Babylonian training academy for government service under the charge of the man over the young eunuchs. But Daniel's career was nearly aborted before it started. As Daniel 1 records, there was something unclean about the food served to the young trainees. The Bible does not give us specifics. Daniel's God-given faith, strong conscience and diplomatic acumen are already apparent at his young age. The fact that Daniel had been emasculated took nothing from his courage despite its physical effects. He requested a change in diet for himself and his three Jewish friends in order to avoid violating God's Law concerning food. Naturally, the man in charge feared repercussions if Daniel and his friends looked less healthy than their contemporaries in the training course. Instead of defiance, Daniel proposed a test for 10 days, promising to submit if the substitute diet did not work. Daniel had faith in God that He would make the diet work for him and his three friends. Daniel's faith was rewarded and the changed diet was made permanent.

One might comment that as a eunuch Daniel would not need as much protein and fats as a physically normal boy because he would never develop normal masculine muscle. But Daniel did not rely on natural or medical considerations. Nor is God bound by them, as the profusion of miracle healings performed by Jesus Christ proves. The most basic lesson is that Daniel was willing to obey God even in a hostile environment and even after severe trauma. This trait was to re-appear many years later after the Persians had conquered the Babylonians. In God's providence Daniel and his three friends were in better health than their fellow students, so their diet in compliance with Jewish law was made permanent.

A major doctrinal lesson is that genuine faith (a gift of God—see Philippians 1:29 and Ephesians 2:8-10) will in time bring obedience to God in its train. James instructs us that *"Faith without works is dead."* (James 2:26) In Matthew 13, our Lord Jesus in His great Parable of the Soils (more commonly called the Parable of the Sower, but I think that is a misnomer) called only one type of soil good—the type that bore fruit. Luke 13:6-9 contains the Parable of the Fig Tree. In this parable God does show patience—He gave the fig tree one more year to bear fruit. But the conclusion cannot be escaped: a tree (or a person or even the nation of Israel in the time of Jesus Christ) who remains fruitless shall be cut down. In this same vein consider John 15:5-6. *"He [or she] that abides in Me bears much fruit, for without Me you can do nothing. If a man (or a woman) does not abide in Me, he [or she] is cast forth as a branch. Men gather them and they are burned."* Faith and fruit-bearing go together because the person of faith abides in Christ Jesus.

The immediate, practical evidence of the fruit-bearing of Daniel and of his three friends was apparent at graduation time. King Nebuchadnezzar himself administered oral exams. Daniel was at the top of the class with his three friends also showing outstanding performances. As a result, all four were assigned to the central administration instead of being farmed out to the provinces. As the sequel shows, Daniel developed a close friendship with King Nebuchadnezzar and Nebuchadnezzar trusted Daniel despite his foreign and captive origins. But this trust did not mature slowly but rather was forged in a crisis.

QUESTIONS FOR REFLECTION AND DISCUSSION

1. How was Daniel loyal to the Babylonians after they had castrated him? Can this be attributed solely to the physical and hormonal effects of the operation? Why did he not either grieve to excess or become resentful? Did Daniel forgive his captors?

2. His castration made Daniel unfit to worship in the Temple. Yet Daniel maintained his faith even though God did not spare him from castration. Did Daniel understand at this early age that the castration was part of God's plan for him? Were the physical effects of the castration a factor in preserving Daniel from immediate death about 70 years later when the Media-Persian alliance overpowered Babylon?

3. Daniel was apparently the valedictorian of his graduating class. In chapter 6 we see that he was still "the smartest man in the room" nearly 70 years later. How and why did Daniel stay so mentally vigorous for so long? What was the part of divine grace? What measures did Daniel take or avoid to meet his human responsibilities?

CHAPTER 6 —
Daniel's First Crisis—A summary of Daniel 2

Scholars believe that King Nebuchadnezzar was about 18 years old when he took the throne of Babylon. This would be similar to Alexander the Great. Early in his reign Nebuchnezzar had a terrifying dream that he could neither remember nor understand. But he expected his magicians to be able to solve the mystery. Understandably, they complained that they could not be expected to interpret a dream of which they knew nothing. They asked King Nebuchadnezzar to relate the dream and then they would interpret it. Nebuchadnezzar was smart beyond his years in the ways of oracles and of bureaucracy. He realized that if he supplied the dream that the magicians would concoct an interpretation and play for time until the matter had been forgotten. Nebuchadnezzar demanded genuine miraculous performance. If the magicians could not relate both the dream and the interpretation, they would not only be replaced but executed. Daniel and his three friends were among those marked for execution even though Daniel had not heard the challenge.

This incident gives us a character portrait of the early King Nebuchadnezzar. Like Henry VIII of England, he was imperious and accepted no excuses for failure. In Henry's case the job of his queen was to deliver a male heir. In Nebuchadnezzar's case he demanded that his magicians know a dream that he did not describe. Nebuchadnezzar showed a volcanic temper when his magicians pleaded inability and asked for time. He could be unreasonable and demand the impossible. Many leaders have accomplished much by demanding what appears to be impossible, but his magicians (although worshipers of false gods) were right in saying that what Nebuchadnezzar was demanding was beyond human ability. (Daniel 2:10-11) But Nebuchadnezzar had a point to the extent that the magicians were claiming the ability to communicate with their gods. Were they frauds, as were Baal's priests on Mount Carmel? Nebuchadnezzar was putting them to the acid test and he would soon find out who really was in touch with the true and living God. But we should not imagine that Nebuchadnezzar absorbed the lesson all at once, either intellectually or emotionally. It took many years—we will come back to this when we analyze Daniel 4.

We also get a character portrait of Daniel and his three friends, starting in Daniel 2:14. When Daniel was swept into the maelstrom, he did not flee danger. He went to Arioch, the executioner, instead. In God's mercy and through Daniel's openness Arioch gave Daniel time, that critical resource in so many battles both military and spiritual. **If one of us had a 24-hour stay of execution, how would we use it?** Daniel used his to have a **prayer meeting** with his three friends. Having prayed, then Daniel went to sleep not knowing if or how he would be delivered from the death sentence hanging over his head—and all for not being able to relate and interpret a dream that only the King had experienced and could not remember. Neither would King Nebuchnezzar have told the dream if he could have remembered it.

How many of us would sleep in these circumstances? Daniel did as Peter did in Acts 12 the night before he was supposed to be executed. Peter slept soundly enough that the angel hit him to wake him up; Daniel slept soundly enough that God gave Daniel Nebuchadnezzar's secret in a dream. Of course Daniel arranged to enter the king's presence and tell him the dream and the interpretation. Many lives were spared as a result, and King Nebuchadnezzar went so far as to prostrate himself before Daniel for the moment, which was excessive because only God is to be worshiped. (Daniel 2:46) Daniel's three friends were promoted within the province of Babylon (the homeland and most important province, probably like the Russian provincial government of the old U.S.S.R. compared to the All-Union central government). Daniel himself stayed in the presence of the king, the highest echelon of all. But Nebuchnezzar, despite his momentary reaction to worship Daniel, remained a proud absolute monarch whose ultimate god was himself.

King Nebuchadnezzar's dream was the first unfolding of God's plan for the Middle East for the several centuries from that time until the coming of Messiah, Whom we know as Jesus Christ (the Greek word Christ is the exact equivalent of the Hebrew Messiah). We now know that the vision from the rise of Babylon to the collapse of the Roman Empire in the West lasted over 1000 years, and over 2000 years if one considers the Byzantine Empire to be the continuation of the Roman Empire. This first vision and the others that follow in Daniel all show the pattern of four dominant empires.

King Nebuchadnezzar's dream had one massive figure with a head of gold (Nebuchadnezzar himself), shoulders and arms of silver (Media-Persia, which was the ruling power during the times of Haggai, Zechariah, Malachi, Ezra, Nehemiah and Esther), a core of bronze (symbolizing Greek rule, which in truth divided into four powers) and then the legs of iron, answering to the Roman Empire which ruled politically during the life of Jesus Christ in His body like ours. Opinions may differ as to the meaning of the toes, where the iron and clay are together without being truly coherent. The Roman Empire for centuries was "partly strong and partly broken." The Byzantine Empire remained strong in the East while the West fell apart. Some also view this as a picture of the old Roman world (especially in Western Europe) at the verge of the return of our Lord. If so, modern times would fit the description well.

From the progression of metals, the standard of excellence seems to decline with time. King Nebuchadnezzar indeed stands above Alexander the Great in terms of longevity and self-control (Alexander the Great, humanly speaking, died young from the effects of excessive drinking as much as from any other cause, although his constant military campaigns did not permit enough rest either). After Cyrus the Great, the quality of Persian kings did fall off even as Persian power peaked. The Greek rulers of Syria (the Seleucids) eventually persecuted the Jews and their fall opened the way for Herod the Great, who ruled with Roman support. As bad as Herod was, the Roman Emperors Caligula and Nero were far worse. The general pattern in King Nebuchadnezzar's prophetic dream was true by history.

But the most important part of the dream was the finish shown in Daniel 2:44. In truth in the days of the Roman kings a new kingdom was established that will never die but will destroy all others. This is the Kingdom of Jesus the Messiah, prophesied by King David earlier in Psalm 45 and referred to in Hebrews 1:8 and 7:1 and throughout the Gospels, especially Matthew. The Lord Jesus spoke of the Kingdom of Heaven, or sometimes the Kingdom of God. Once again history proves the dream to have been true. Christianity, based on the Holy Scriptures, was founded during Roman rule and has continued ever since in the face of unrelenting opposition from every quarter. Through the centuries Christians have been martyred by nearly every major political power known to history since His death. Educated and illiterate people have this in common: that their civilizations have resisted Jesus Christ and have often killed His emissaries because they refused to even listen to His message. Even where Christianity has taken root, its true disciples have rarely formed a majority of the population. Jesus the Messiah indeed promised that *"on this rock [Peter's profession that Jesus is the Messiah, the Son of the living God] I will build My Church, and the gates of hell shall not prevail against it."* Matthew 16:18. But He also warned, *"You shall be hated of all nations for My name's sake."* Matthew 24:9. As Daniel and his three friends were a tiny minority in a pagan government with a king still pagan at heart, so we are a minority in a hostile world today. We are part of a tiny slice of the proof of Nebuchadnezzar's dream and of the truth of the words of Jesus Christ. Peter in 2 Peter 3:9 said that we are *"a chosen generation, a royal priesthood, a chosen nation, a peculiar people (often translated as a people for His own possession), to show forth the praises of Him Who has called us out of darkness into His marvelous light."*

I will not attempt here a complete exposition of the Book of Revelation nor of the Kingdom of Jesus Christ of which every believer is a citizen. I have wrestled with aspects of Revelation in my previous book *Fight to the Finish,* published by Trafford Press in 2011. Many other authors have made more substantial contributions to understanding it. But for present purposes the over-arching theme of Revelation is the detailed exposition of the complete, permanent, total and final triumph of Jesus Christ over all enemies. Presently, as in Hebrews 2:8, we *"do not yet see all things put under Him."* But Hebrews 1 and 2 in showing the absolute superiority and Deity of Jesus Christ explains that this will happen. Revelation 20:10 records the final destruction and judgment of the Devil. Colossians 1 and 2:14-15 deal with other aspects of the triumph of the Kingdom of the Messiah over all others. In 1 Corinthians 15:25-26, we read that *"for He must reign until He has put all enemies under His feet. The last enemy to be destroyed is death."*

QUESTIONS FOR REFLECTION AND DISCUSSION:

1. Suppose King Nebuchadnezzar were transported in time to be the CEO of a major international corporation today. What would be his strengths and weaknesses from a business and then from a Biblical perspective?
2. When trouble arises in your life, how quick are you to pray?
3. How much comfort do you derive from the smashing of the image by the Stone in Daniel 2:44?

CHAPTER 7 —
The Second Crisis (Daniel 3)

Nebuchadnezzar did not follow up on his confession in Daniel 2:47 *"Truly your God is a God of gods, a Lord of kings and a revealer of secrets."* He would have avoided much misery if he had lived by that profession. But the struggle between King Nebuchadnezzar and God Himself had only started. Nebuchadnezzar seized upon his place as the head of gold in the image of his dream to justify making a gigantic golden image of himself and ordering everyone to worship the image at the sound of the music. Instead of glorifying God he glorified himself.

Pride lay at the root of Nebuchadnezzar's orders to construct the image and then to have his officials worship it. If one looks at Isaiah 14:12-14, one finds that Lucifer (Satan) says "I will" five times. Satan personifies pride. As James says, *"God resists the proud but gives grace to the humble. Shortly after James said, "Humble yourselves in the sight of the Lord, and He shall lift you up."* (James 4:6, 10) Satan will never humble himself for all eternity, even though he will perpetually endure eternal damnation in hellfire. Satan will eventually admit that Jesus is Lord (Philippians 2:10-11) but because of his pride he will continuously rebel in his heart and mind in the Lake of Fire. At this time of his life Nebuchadnezzar was of a similar frame of mind. He misused the knowledge and blessing of God's message through the dream to exalt himself. For seven years he lost his authority. It nearly cost him both life and eternity.

Nebuchadnezzar's pride, expressed in the construction of the golden image, brought him into a collision with Almighty God. As Solomon, a wise king, warned in Proverbs 15:25, *"The Lord will destroy the house of the proud."* Proverbs 6:17 lists *"a proud look"* as the first of seven things that the Lord hates. *"Everyone proud in heart is an abomination to the Lord."* Proverbs 16:5. *"A high look, a proud heart and the plowing of the wicked are sin."* Proverbs 21:4. *"Pride goes before destruction, and a haughty spirit before a fall."* Proverbs 16:18. *"Pride, arrogance and the perverse [using the ASV rendering] mouth I [God] hate.* Proverbs 8:13. *"A man's pride will bring him low, but he that is of a lowly spirit shall obtain honor.* Proverbs 29:23. Much later 1 John 2:16 was written: *"For all that is in the world: the lust of the flesh, the lust of the eyes and the pride of life is not of the Father but is of the world."*

When Daniel's three friends refused to worship the image, some God-hating official saw an opportunity to get rid of three able rivals within the bureaucracy. So that person informed on Daniel's three friends. At first Nebuchadnezzar somewhat restrained his temper and allowed them a second chance to conform, although Nebuchadnezzar also challenged any god to deliver Daniel's three friends (v. 15). But Daniel's three friends had made no mistake but chose to obey the First and Second Commandments rather than Nebuchadnezzar's worship orders. They told Nebuchadnezzar that God was able to deliver them if He chose; if not, they would rather die than worship the image notwithstanding Nebuchadnezzar's orders. At this Nebuchadnezzar completely lost his temper and not only ordered the three friends into the furnace but also ordered the furnace to be heated seven times its normal temperature. This was irrational. The normal temperature would have been ample to kill Daniel's three friends. Nebuchadnezzar was expressing his volcanic anger without restraint. The result was that some of his best soldiers were burned to death in the process of heaving Daniels' three friends into the furnace. In giving such an order Nebuchadnezzar is an example of the truth of James 3:6: *"And the tongue is a fire, a world of iniquity. So is the tongue among our body parts, that it defiles the whole body and sets on fire the course of nature, and it is set on fire from hell."* The overheated furnace is a picture of the consequences of thoughtless words and is also a picture of human nature without transformation through Jesus Christ. The Lord Jesus Himself taught that *"Those things which proceed out of the mouth come forth from the heart, and they defile a man."* Matthew 15:18. Nebuchadnezzar here is an example of an intelligent and energetic leader defiled by his sinful, wicked nature as expressed by his order to burn Daniel's three friends in the superheated furnace.

It is also fair to consider the superheated furnace a picture of the Lake of Fire and of the hellfire that our Lord Jesus mentioned in several passages. One is Matthew 5:22; see also Matthew 5:29-30 for a similar usage. The superheated furnace had no power over Daniel's three friends and similar the Lake of Fire has no power over believers. Revelation 20:6.

Yet God in His patience gave Nebuchadnezzar another sign before bringing any sort of judgment upon him. Daniel's three friends were unharmed by the superheated furnace. Their clothes were not even burned! Not only that, there was a fourth Man in the furnace. Nebuchadnezzar even perceived this Man as being "like the Son of God" (v.25, KJV). I recognize that some translations use "a son of the gods," but the Hebrew (or perhaps Chaldee) is *el-aw* and not the plural *elohim*. I see no textual basis for the plural "gods" even though literary license would assume that Nebuchadnezzar would have used a plural word because of his polytheistic background. King Nebuchadnezzar already knew in his mind from Daniel's ability to relate and interpret his dream that there is but one true God—the God of Israel—and that knowledge forced its way to the forefront under the pressure of this second major miracle. Nebuchadnezzar made it a capital offense to curse the God of Israel (Daniel 3:29), but as we shall see he did not yet worship Him from the heart. Yet God in His grace and mercy remained patient and continued to use Nebuchadnezzar to shelter His exiled Jews. This shelter was reflected in the next vision of Nebuchadnezzar as a gigantic tree sheltering many birds and animals.

Who was the fourth person in the furnace? King Nebuchadnezzar did not know but did say that the fourth person appeared "like the

Son of God." A search of the Old Testament enables us to identify the fourth person as the Son of God before He took on human flesh and became Jesus Christ. Genesis 1:26 and 3:22 make it clear that the Creator was plural rather than singular, even though there is one true God. Isaiah 48:16 indicates three persons in the single Godhead. Hosea 12:3-4 and Genesis 32:24-30 indicate that Jacob wrestled with a Man, but that Man is also identified as an angel—the same Angel of the Lord that was worshiped in Judges 13. Psalm 2:12 warns everyone to *"Kiss the Son, lest He be angry and you perish in the way, when His wrath is kindled but a little. Blessed are all they who put their trust in Him."* This is a clear command to worship the Son—the Son of God is not merely an extraordinary human being. He is equal to the Father and equally to be worshiped. (See also John 5:17-27 for confirmation.) Genesis 17 and 18 both state that the Lord appeared to Abraham. Obviously the Father did not leave the heavens, but rather He sent His Son in an angelic body that appeared human (as the angels' bodies also appeared human to the homosexuals of Sodom in Genesis 19). So Nebuchadnezzar was on the right track when he spoke of the Son of God in the furnace. It was the Son of God as He lived before taking human flesh Who was in the furnace. As we shall see later, Daniel was able to distinguish between the Son of God and subordinate angels that he sent in later visions.

Are you in a figurative furnace? If you are, this passage is for you. It is hard to imagine a more desperate situation than being thrown into a hot furnace, perhaps hot enough to make steel. Or imagine being locked into a shower at a Nazi death camp. Daniel's three friends were toast! And yet through the power of God they came through the fire smelling like a rose. Not even their clothes smelled of smoke. God delivered Corrie ten Boom from Ravensbruck. He can deliver us from anything.

Yet we know from experience that God does not always to choose to deliver us from tribulation or certain death. Hebrews 11:35-8 comes immediately after the account of the heroes of faith. *"Others were tortured, not accepting deliverance, that they might obtain a better resurrection. And others had trials of mocking and scourging, and yes, moreover of bonds and imprisonment. They were stoned; they were sawed in half, were tempted, were killed with the sword. They wandered about in sheepskins and goatskins, being destitute, afflicted, tormented (of whom the world was not worthy). They wandered in deserts, in mountains and in caves of the earth."* We do know that for those who endure such treatment that God's promise has not failed. Daniel's three friends survived and were promoted. Others may have lost the life of our present bodies, but they were still delivered. Our Lord Jesus promised the church at Smyrna, *"Be faithful to death, and I will give you a crown of life."* Revelation 2:10. The foremost of those who suffered instead of receiving immediate deliverance is the Lord Jesus Himself. His Father did not permit the cup of suffering to pass from His Son, but delivered His Son through the suffering into a everlasting kingdom forever. As Philippians 2:5-11 teaches, from the suffering Jesus Christ received the *"name that is above every name, that at the name of Jesus every knee shall bow."* Suffering for Christ's sake can be borne because the suffering has eternal purpose. Consider carefully the words of the Lord Jesus in Matthew 19:29, where what may be lost on earth is promised 100-fold in heaven. Whether we triumph or suffer and even die for His sake, Jesus Christ is with us always, just as Matthew 28:20 says. For example, the risen Jesus Christ stood up (Acts 7:55-56) as Stephen was finishing his witness, which ended in his death. Like Pastor Don den Hartog, I believe that our Lord was standing in salute of His faithful deacon.

QUESTIONS FOR REFLECTION & DISCUSSION:

1. Shakespeare wrote that "cowards die many times before their death; the valiant never taste of death but once." Were Daniel's three friends afraid to die?
2. Bravery and courage have been highly prized in American history. What is the public perception of their value today?

What do we make, individually and as churches, of 2 Peter 1:5: *add to your faith valor* . . . (virtue in the King James, but this usage of "virtue" is in the old Renaissance sense of courage or valor according to Strong's Concordance. John Bunyan in *Pilgrim's Progress* understood this when he named one of his heroes "Valiant-for-the-Truth"). How do we in the 21st century stack up against Daniel's three friends or the heroes of faith in Hebrews 11?

3. The Son of God entered the furnace with Daniel's three friends. Do we believe the promise of Matthew 28:20 from Jesus Christ that *"I will be with you always . . ."*?

CHAPTER 8 —
The Humbling and Saving of
Nebuchadnezzar (Daniel 4)

Once more Nebuchadnezzar had a dream that he did not understand. This time he remembered and told Daniel the dream. Over the years Nebuchadnezzar had built up sufficient trust in Daniel that he did not withhold this dream to prove the genuineness of the interpretation. Even having been supplied with the dream, the other "wise men" failed to supply the interpretation. As Nebuchadnezzar expected, Daniel interpreted the dream honestly even though the dream was a warning of trouble ahead for the King. Daniel told the truth and did not show fear the consequences or permit fear to influence his advice. At the time Nebuchadnezzar appeared to be at the zenith of his power. Indeed the Jews and other nations had a measure of prosperity under his rule. Like Napoleon many centuries later, Nebuchandezzar was willing to let a man of foreign origin rise as high as his talents would permit. Daniel and his three Jewish friends were examples. In fact this dream was a warning from God that Nebuchadnezzar would be dethroned and isolated because of his sin (Daniel 4:23-27). Then twelve months later Nebuchnezzar boasted in his heart that he had build Babylon with its magnificent walls, hanging gardens and other wonderful buildings. The same proud spirit that Satan showed in Isaiah 14 appeared again in King Nebuchadnezzar, and this time God's sentence was swift.

"Pride goes before destruction, and a haughty spirit before a fall." Proverbs 16:18. King Nebuchadnezzar lost his throne and his mind

and was driven into a pasture where he ate grass like an ox. He lacked enough reason to take care of his body, so that his body hair resembled eagles' feathers and his nails grew like eagles' claws. His personal hygiene must have been non-existent. His clothes must have been tattered. No doubt his body stank to high heaven. These conditions lasted for 7 years. And this man was the titled King! We are not told that Nebuchadnezzar went about naked, but in many ways his condition was similar to the Gadarene man who lived in the tombs whom Jesus Christ freed from many demons. (Luke 8:26-33). Nobody had any hope or desire that Nebuchadnezzar should be restored. For practical purposes, Nebuchadnezzar was toast!

But as God had delivered Daniel's three friends years before when there was no visible means of deliverance, so now God delivered Nebuchadnezzar as symbolized in the dream by the life shooting up from the stump of the fallen tree. The King came to understand that he was not sovereign; rather God is absolutely sovereign over all people. No more did King Nebuchadnezzar believe that he had built Babylon or that he was an object of worship. The transformation was so complete that Nebuchadnezzar actually composed Daniel 4 as his testimony to the sovereignty and mercy of God when his reason was restored. He also was restored to his kingly power. Daniel 4 was a state paper that Daniel preserved as part of his prophetic writing, but Nebuchadnezzar was its author. Daniel preserved the record for posterity. Leaving aside the question of the authorship of Job, this is the only portion of Old Testament Scripture of which I am aware was written by a Gentile.

God destroyed Nebuchadnezzar's pride and reduced him to the level of an animal, and yet God restored him to the highest heights possible on earth when Nebuchadnezzar finally acknowledged God's rule (Daniel 4:32-36). *"God resists the proud but gives grace to the humble."* James 4:6. Nebuchadnezzar proves both parts of this statement true in a single life. Secular history indicates that Nebuchadnezzar reigned 46 years and died shortly after he wrote Daniel 4. Apparently Nebuchadnezzar died in true faith at his end.

I may be writing to an autocratic entrepreneur who like Nebuchadnezzar thinks that he or she has created a great enterprise. God delivered Nebuchadnezzar from his own pride, and He can equally deliver you from yours. One would hope that the methods could be gentler, but I plead that you ask God to change you from autocrat to servant of the Most High God and of Jesus Christ His Son, whatever it takes.

QUESTIONS FOR REFLECTION & DISCUSSION:

1. What are your personal observations of the destructiveness of pride?

2. Consider the pattern in Scripture. When the Assyrians taunted King Hezekiah that no god could deliver him, what happened to that Assyrian army (see 2 Kings 19:9-13 for the challenge to God and the entire chapter for the answer)? What happened to Nebuchadnezzar when he ignored God in his thinking? What happened to the sorcerer when he tried to impede the Holy Spirit working through Paul and Barnabas in Acts 13:6-12? And what will happen to the Anti-Christ? We may believe these things intellectually, which is important. Do we believe them emotionally as well?

3. Most Jews in Jesus' time tended to assume that all suffering was a result of specific sin (for example, John 9:1-3) At least 3 of Job's companions did the same. The modern tendency is to believe that there never is a relationship between sin and suffering. Is either extreme Scriptural? How do we avoid being judgmental and also avoid the pitfall of ignoring the Biblical teaching that God sometimes judges particular sins with chastening (for example, Hebrews 12) or suffering or even physical death (for example, King Saul, Ananias and Sapphira in Acts 5:1-11, and 1 Corinthians 11:20-34 concerning the abuse of the Lord's Table)?

CHAPTER 9 —
Daniel in Eclipse (Daniel 5)

Secular history records that the power of Babylon began to wane after Nebuchadnezzar's death. Certainly his successors were nowhere near the quality of Nebuchadnezzar as a ruler. Belshazzar was in charge, although not officially the top ruler, when the Book of Daniel resumes its narrative history about 24 years after Nebuchadnezzar's death. At this point a cycle of 70 years from Daniel's initial captivity had run. Babylon was under siege, but Belshazzar was unconcerned. He was having a riotous, drunken party, feeling secure behind the ramparts with a secure food and water supply sufficient to outlast a besieging army. A military man would point out that such a party would sap the morale of the sentries on the front line. This is true, but Belshazzar's troubles ran beyond human military concerns. He was praising all sorts of false gods and then had decided to insult the true God by having the revelers drink from the vessels that had been removed from the Temple by Nebuchadnezzar's armies years before.

It is obvious that Daniel had been forgotten. The only person who remembered him was the "queen", which I believe should be understood to be the queen mother, either Nebuchadnezzar's widow or a daughter or another elderly woman in Nebuchadnezzar's family. (Daniel 5:10) She was of a bygone generation. Belshazzar's cronies were not familiar with Daniel and would not have appreciated his wisdom had they known him.

The revelers loved to drink alcohol and get wasted. They loved false gods—idols. With both men and women together (and especially concubines) there was probably a sexual undertone to the gathering.

Daniel would have nothing to do with any of that. No wonder he was not there. In fact, God Himself was crashing this party and Daniel as God's representative prophet would pronounce its doom and the death sentence upon Belshazzar.

The only reason why Daniel was dusted off and summoned to the party was the original "handwriting on the wall." Belshazzar's mood had changed from rowdy drunkenness to sheer terror—he probably felt portents of doom even without understanding the words, and so he lost control of his legs and trembled when he saw a part of a hand and words that he did not understand: *mene, mene, tekel, upharsin (plural of peres)." * Daniel explained: *"MENE: God has numbered your kingdom and brought it to an end. TEKEL: You have been weighed and have been found deficient. PERES: Your kingdom is divided and given to the Medes and Persians."* Daniel 5:25-28. The Scriptures record Belshazzar's death and the end of the Babylonian regime that very night (Daniel 5:30). The Greek historian Heroditus, whose writings are not fully inspired Scripture but which are usually reliable, records that the Media-Persian coalition dammed the river, marched down the dry riverbed and took advantage of the intoxicated condition of the guards to gain entry into the city and kill Belshazzar. This story rings true given the logical effects of the drunken orgy of the leadership upon the fighting troops at the immediate front. The Babylonian Empire was dead—the head of gold in Daniel's first vision was gone.

But what of Daniel? Despite his initial refusal of King Belshazzar's honors, Daniel had been named the third ruler of the kingdom and given clothing and insignia to match. Normally, he would have been a prime target for the conquering coalition army of Media-Persia. But instead the conquerors restored Daniel's authority even beyond what it had been when Nebuchadnezzar was in his prime, despite Daniel's advanced age (70 years of captivity plus his age when originally captured). He was one of 3 presidents over the provincial administrators and then was promoted over all those administrators. The governing powers were considering turning over the whole administration to

Daniel. This is testimony to the tremendous God-given skill that Daniel brought to government and to his integrity. It is also testimony to the mighty power of God that controls the hearts and minds of people, especially people of power. *The heart of the king is in the hand of the Lord as rivers of water. He turns it wheresoever He wills.* Proverbs 21:1. In modern times, we do have the example of Robert Gates, who served as Secretary of Defense under both George W. Bush and Barack Obama. His example is quite remarkable, but still it does not compare to Daniel's service in the Babylonian government followed by his recall to authority by the military conquerors of Babylon.

In my judgment, Daniel is the greatest Secretary of the Treasury or Chancellor of the Exchequer that has ever served in any government. He passed every audit; nobody could find fault with his work. (Daniel 6:4) I believe that Daniel started a tradition of Jewish statesmanship in the service of nations that still continues. Later under the Persians, Mordecai as related in the Book of Esther and Nehemiah are people who followed Daniel in this respect. Maimonides served as a personal physician to Muslim rulers in Egypt. In the 20th century Bernard Baruch was an example of a counselor to several presidents in the United States. On at least one occasion he also prevented Winston Churchill from becoming insolvent at the start of the Great Depression. An earlier example was the original Joseph in Egypt, but there is no direct historical continuity between Joseph and Daniel.

Before we move forward to the time of Media-Persia, we can learn from looking back at the 70 years from Nebuchadnezzar's first entry into Jerusalem to Belshazzar's death. Nebuchadnezzar's first dream spanned several hundred years. In identifying the gold head with Nebuchadnezzar the first dream forecast a bright future for Babylon as long as he lived—which indeed proved to be true. In a different dream related in chapter 7 (but dated from the first year of Belshazzar) Babylonia is portrayed as a lion, originally with wings for speed to be combined with the strength of the lion but later diminished by the removal of the wings. Clearly the agility of Babylon under

Nebuchadnezzar ceased as prophesied during Belshazzar's terminal reign. Then in chapter 4, Nebuchnezzar relates his second dream which warned of his own downfall and left room for his restoration. But the judgment of this downfall was stayed for 12 months and Daniel pleaded with Nebuchadnezzar to change his ways (Daniel 4:27) in the hope that God would relent—as He had with Nineveh in the days of Jonah. But Nebuchadnezzar did not heed and the judgment fell, although it was not final either in the dream or in real life. In contrast, Belshazzar at the orgy was not given any time or opportunity to repent. Daniel pronounced judgment, which came that night. Belshazzar's terror and doom might be compared to King Saul after he visited the witch at En-Dor (1 Samuel 28:5-25).

In both cases the men had crossed a line against God from which there was no return. As mere human beings we must remember that we are part of His Creation and subject to His Laws. While every human being except Jesus Christ has transgressed, some people provoke God to immediate and irremediable anger by deliberate sin. Every one of us should pray for the restraining of the Holy Spirit lest we become like them. It is awful enough even for one whom God has ultimately chosen to save—like Nebuchadnezzar with his pride or Samson with his lust—to provoke God to severe corrective measures. But not even that compares with the awful everlasting judgments facing people like Belshazzar and Saul who trigger His eternal anger. *It is a fearful thing to fall into the hands of the living God.* Hebrews 10:31 (I would recommend considering Hebrews 10:26-31 as a whole.)

The old balance of power system that had existed from the time of Joshua was gone for good. With the fall of Babylon, the first of the great powers that would rule the Holy Land was likewise gone. Like Babylon, Media-Persia rose from the east of the Promised Land. The later two powers—Greece and Rome—would arise from the west. The last power, and the only survivor, would be the Kingdom of God itself. We will tackle this in more detail when we consider Daniel 7. Before we do that, we will follow that story of Daniel himself in chapter 6.

CHAPTER 10 —
Daniel's crisis in the service of
Media-Persia (Daniel 6)

As we have already seen, Daniel made rapid progress in his career under the Median ruler named or titled Darius. But as we often experience today, the Devil is displeased when God's people progress and a confrontation often results. So it was with Daniel.

The other officials were jealous of Daniel's rise but could find no legitimate professional criticism. But this did not deter them from trying to take Daniel down. So they searched for a way to attack Daniel because he was "different." They found this place in Daniel's worship of the God of Israel. Daniel 6:5 sums up their thought process: *"Then said these men, 'We shall not find any occasion against this Daniel except we find against him concerning the law of his God.'"* But at this time there was nothing illegal about Daniel worshiping the God of Israel. So this sinister cabal decided to change that.

Before proceeding with the narrative, we can observe once again the destructiveness of pride. These bureaucrats could have served under Daniel, recognizing his superiority and his fitness for the authority he had been given. This would have been their proper course. In terms of historical analogy, I am reminded of a British officer in India named Baird who was miffed because he thought he was in line for a command that was instead given to Arthur Wellesley. Years later that officer recognized and testified that his superiors were right and that he was wrong to have been irritated. He considered it an honor to at one time have been weighed for the same responsible command as Wellesley. Baird can be said to have realized his proper level. The young Arthur Wellesley who had surpassed Baird in India was later known as the Duke of Wellington, the general who defeated Napoleon and who later became the Prime Minister of England. In swallowing his pride, Baird actually won an important victory within his own soul. *He that is slow to anger is better than the mighty, and he that rules a spirit [is better] than he that takes a city.* Proverbs 16:32. The Duke of Wellington also was an outstanding example of the power of self-control in a life. But these rivals of Daniel were overwhelmed with pride and envy and applied what self-control they had to a diabolical scheme rather than submit willingly to honest management. On a lesser scale, we see rivalries today within large companies and modern governments like that between Daniel and the other bureaucrats, although the stakes usually are not as drastic as they were for Daniel.

Being consumed with pride themselves, Daniel's enemies knew how to appeal to the pride of Darius. They proposed a law that declared it a capital crime to pray to anyone except Darius himself for 30 days. They knew that Daniel would never wait that long to pray to God. They persuaded Darius to rush the law through without reflection and especially without giving Daniel an opportunity to give his advice. So in effect it became illegal to worship God, and it was not long before the plotters went to Daniel's house and caught him in the act of prayer and dragged him before Darius. Daniel had become aware of the law but continued his practice of prayer three times each day. As Peter said later to the Jewish Sanhedrin, *"We ought to obey God rather than men."* Acts 5:29. Darius now realized his grave error but it was too late. Once again Daniel was as good as dead, having been thrown into a dungeon with hungry lions inside.

QUESTIONS FOR REFLECTION AND DISCUSSION:

1. Is prayer important enough for you to be willing to die for it?
2. How willing are you in your work, home or church to submit to honest leadership?
3. In speaking of the Lord's Table, the Scriptures teach, *"But let a man examine himself and so eat of that bread and drink of that cup."* 1 Corinthians 11:28. Are you willing to examine yourself honestly? Are you willing with King David to pray to God to *"Search me, and know my heart; try me and know my thoughts, and see if there is any wicked way in me . . ."* Psalm 139:23-24
4. We are often justly critical of government action taken in haste, especially when legislators have not had time to even read or study the legislation. This often happens at the end of sessions because of procrastination before. But what about you? Have you made hasty decisions under the pressure of your own desire or under the pressure of some salesperson who knows the power of haste in overcoming sensible objections?
5. Do you get so angry that even for an instant you want to kill somebody, perhaps someone close to you?

But just as Daniel escaped near-certain death by Nebuchadnezzar's decree in chapter 2 and his three friends survived the superheated furnace in chapter 3, Daniel again is spared through no power of his own but by divine intervention of God Almighty. When Daniel (6:22) told Darius that *"God has sent His angel"* to stop the lions from harming him, I cannot say from the text whether this was a standard angel or the specific Angel of the Lord that represents the Son of God before He took human flesh. Either way, God's intervention was effective and Daniel lived on to the long life span that God had appointed. *"This poor man cried, and the Lord delivered him out of all of his troubles."* Psalm 34:6.

6. It has been said of a few coaches and military leaders that their men would go through a wall for them. Do you feel that way about God? This sounds hard, but through what did Jesus Christ go for you?

7. Have you been delivered from apparent disaster? If you have, have you thanked God?

8. Can you draw joy from the promises of God that He will deliver you from all of your present and future troubles, no matter how fearful they seem now?

While writing this, I had a dream that helped me understand the importance of the Persian insistence that the king was subject fully to Persian law. One can criticize rightly a system so rigid that no amendment to existing law was possible, but to give the power of amendment to the king alone would make the king's power arbitrary and unlimited. The Persians at least realized that there had to be some way to limit a fallible king's authority. The provision that the king was bound by law was an important first step. In later English history, this issue was opened in 1215 at the Magna Carta and not finally settled until the expulsion of King James II from English soil after the Battle of the Boyne in 1691.

The dream may seem to be remote from the subject, but I am constrained to relate it. Some of my readers may not understand baseball well. Please bear with me. God was teaching me with an illustration that I would understand so that I can pass it on to you. I claim no independent authority for my dream nor my understanding of it. Like all things, this must be tested by the Holy Scriptures and must be strictly subordinate to them.

In my dream I was playing first base in the 5th inning of a baseball game. Somehow I was player-manager for a youth team with a number of minority players. We led by 1 run. The other team was at bat with the bases loaded, and we had succeeded in getting the 2nd out against a good hitter. Another good hitter was at bat. This batter hit a sharp ground ball to the right side. My instinctive move was back to first base, figuring that the 2nd baseman would field it. Then I realized to my dismay that the ball was going through to right field. The thought flashed that I had chickened out on attempting to reach and field the grounder and then I moved to a cut-off position. I could see that the runner starting from first was vulnerable going to third, so I cut off the throw and threw to the third baseman in ample time to get that runner and at least get out of the inning. He applied the tag at least 18 inches short of third base, and then that umpire called the runner safe.

The third baseman gave a questioning look at the umpire and the umpire ejected him. So far as I could tell he had not said a word. When I ran over to the umpire to find out what was going on, the ump just said that he thought it was better to call the runner safe and added that he had not only ejected my third baseman but also fined him $2000.00, even though he was but a youth. (Of course an umpire cannot do that in real life, but this is part of the point of the dream.) I called my team off the field, telling my third basemen to repeat my call in Spanish for those players who might be unsure of my meaning in English. I told the umpire and then my team that we cannot and would not play when the umpires themselves were not willing to be subject to the rules of baseball. I explained to my team that we would have to find another league where the rules of baseball governed the umpires as well as the players. We cannot play where the umpires are going to be arbitrary, favoring whom they feel like at the moment. Now I awoke.

Through this dream God was reminding me that government officers, whether kings, judges or others, must themselves be subject to law because of the common sin of all humanity (excluding Jesus Christ, the Son of God). I believe that many American judges violate this principle when they "make law," claiming the authority to impose their own preferences as distinct from applying existing law or extending the principles of existing law to truly analogous situations. But back to Daniel's time, the Persians had at least recognized the problem of limiting a king's authority by their principle of compelling their kings to submit to existing law. Later in the time of Esther, the king in the name of justice gave the Jews in his realm the right to defend themselves against the *pogrom* that Haman was instigating before his execution, but the king was unable to amend or repeal the earlier murderous law that he had permitted Haman to issue.

Later in the history of the Persian Empire, the principle of precedent was a great help to Israel. When Nehemiah was reconstructing Jerusalem and its walls, he was able to use Cyrus' original decree to overcome opposition from Israel's neighbors. When Cyrus' decree issued during Daniel's lifetime was discovered and confirmed in the archives, the King of Nehemiah's time confirmed the decree and supplied state funds for the project.

But recognizing the need for some limits on a king's authority is not enough to restrain arbitrary power, as the horrible substance of Darius' law shows. Daniel's enemies knew how to flatter and to appeal to Darius' pride, that original sin of the Devil himself. The very idea of prayer, as distinct from a petition, to a sinful, human king is revolting. The idea of forbidding prayer to God, the Creator of the universe, for any length of time is blasphemous. Darius was flattered into claiming superiority over God. From the sequel, Darius was capable of better judgment than that, but this law is a monument to how far pride can warp the judgment of a normally reasonable man.

Now in real life Darius was about to lose his most able administrator because of his foolish pride. He was greatly distressed but could find no legal way out. Therefore he carried out the sentence against Daniel for the "crime" of praying to God. Darius did compel the other officials to share responsibility by affixing their rings to the seal of the den. Then Darius fasted and stayed awake all night, praying that somehow Daniel would escape death in the execution chamber. God did take Darius off the hook and delivered faithful Daniel from otherwise certain death.

Viewed from Daniel's standpoint, God was not finished with him yet. So God did not permit him to die but rather sent an angel to seal the lions' mouths and prevent them from eating or even harming him.

God does not do this on every occasion when one of His children are at the point of an unjust execution. Stephen (Acts 7) died while Daniel was delivered. As a totally and fully sovereign God He does have the power to make decisions that seem arbitrary to us. We will take up the issue posed here of whether God is bound by His own laws or whether He has authority above His Law.

First we should consider the severity of the judgment that fell on those who plotted against Daniel. They suffered the very penalty that they intended for Daniel. "*With whatever measure you judge, you shall be judged. With whatever measure you measure out, it shall be measured back to you again.*" Matthew 7:2. Haman later in Persian history was hanged on his own gallows. Esther 7:10. Darius extended the judgment to the families of the plotters, as the sons of Haman were hanged with their father. Did God command this? No. It is expounded by the prophet Ezekiel in chapter 18 that people are to be judged for their own actions, not for the actions of their fathers. But ancient kings commonly wiped out the families so that nobody in the next generation would be alive to take revenge.

That observation brings us to the issue of whether God is subject to His own law or whether He is free to act or to permit others to act in apparent violation of the principles He requires of us. One instance of this is recorded in 1 Kings 22:22-23 and in 2 Chronicles 18:19-22, where God permitted one of His angels to lie to Ahab's prophets in order to lure Ahab to his death. God also sent a prophet to tell Ahab the truth, but Ahab punished the prophet for his candor. Lying is generally a sin, although war and espionage are exceptions to this principle (see the story of Rahab in Joshua 2 as one example of the exception). In another instance, Haman was hanged (Esther 7) under a mistaken impression that he was trying to rape Esther when in fact he was pleading to Queen Esther for his life. God permitted the King to proceed under this assumption because Haman in fact was worthy of death as the would-be murderer of the Jews, although not as a would-be rapist. God also permitted Satan to harm Job when Job, though a sinner, was devoted to Him and had committed no sin that would ordinarily have provoked God to such severity as Job received. Yet God did not sin in exposing Job to Satan's buffeting; what Satan did was less than the full measure of the punishment of eternal death for any sin.

Romans 9 is probably the strongest statement of God's sovereignty, especially verses 18-23. God has the right to destroy anyone or to permit any of us to be martyred for our faith. We are both subordinate and infinitely inferior to Him. God set the Pharaoh high in order to smash him as a warning to the entire human race not to rebel against Him, following up His earlier warning at the Tower of Babel.

We cannot avoid the issue by referring to the will of man. This too is under God's overall control. We can see that Hitler unwittingly became the midwife of the revived nation of Israel. There would never have been United Nations approval for an independent Israel without the horror of the Holocaust. Why did God use a method to revive Israel that involved so much killing? I cannot answer the question, but I cannot avoid the fact that God could have employed another method to reconstitute Israel but permitted Hitler to run his murderous course instead and then stopped him before all of Europe's Jews were exterminated. (Compare Deuteronomy 7.) I must trust the righteousness and wisdom of God with the questions which I cannot answer.

So can we trust God with His infinite power? Yes! Certainly we cannot trust any sinful human being with such power. The key lies in the perfect, holy character of God. He will not break His covenants with His children even when His children violate the terms of the covenant. Noah promptly got drunk after he got out of the Ark, yet God did not flood the entire earth again as He had promised. He has kept that promise ever since. Samson had his eyes gouged out and yet died a hero. God kept His covenant promises with King David (2 Samuel 7) even in the face of David's terrible sins involving Uriah and Bathsheba (2 Samuel 11-12). God has preserved Israel as a mostly scattered nation from the time of Nebuchadnezzar and Daniel's childhood and since the early 20th century (and especially since 1948) has been starting to restore that nation to its earthly homeland in the face of the provocation of many in Israel against Him. God is totally faithful in his covenants.

Even more, God the Father keeps His promises to His Son, Who in human flesh was Jesus Christ (or Jesus the Messiah). Psalm 2:7-9 reveals a portion of the terms of a decree by the Father in favor of His Son. Hebrews 1 gives more information. It is the Son Himself Who intercedes for His people to the Father (Romans 8:34), ensuring that His death is effective atonement for every one of His elect. The one who has come to Jesus Christ will never be cast out. (John 6:36-40, 10:27-30). There may be severe chastening of a child of God, but never complete disinheritance because of His own decree. We cannot trust ourselves with our salvation; we would never "hang on." But we do not need to trust ourselves but rather our Savior. He hangs on to us. *"It is He that has made us, and not we ourselves. We are His people, and the sheep of His pasture."* Psalm 100:3. *"He that keeps Israel neither slumbers nor sleeps."* Psalm 121:4. So we as believers in Jesus Christ are in the all-powerful hands of a loving Shepherd rather than of a destructive monster like King Kong or a cruel ruler like Dracula. On the other hand, for the unbeliever *"it is a fearful thing to fall into the hands of the living God."* Hebrews 10:31.

QUESTIONS FOR REFLECTION AND DISCUSSION:

1. How readily do you succumb to flattery? Is the tendency to be manipulated by flattery a reflection of pride?
2. Neither Daniel nor his three friends showed fear in the face of death. What is your view of death? Does your emotional reaction match your intellectual view?
3. How much do you feel the love of God as you live your life? Feelings can be deceiving, but is the Lord Jesus a familiar friend or a stranger? How is this reflected in your prayer time?

4. Abraham tried to bargain with God concerning Sodom and Gomorrah. Job was granted his wish for an audience with God—he originally wanted to plead his innocence. Are you intimate enough with God to ask Him questions? Are you submissive enough to accept His answers or to accept His refusal to answer your questions?

CHAPTER 11 —
Daniel's visions during Belshazzar's rule (Daniel 7 & 8)

These visions are presented out of time sequence so that Daniel's history under the Persians could be connected with the fall of Babylon. The four beasts of Daniel 7 is a presentation of the same basic sequence as Nebuchadnezzar's original dream of the one body composed of four different metals. The dream of chapter 8 focuses upon the coming fall of Persia to the Greeks led by Alexander the Great.

The first vision in chapter 7 is in its essence similar to the vision that King Nebuchadnezzar had had when Daniel had just started in government service. The first animal is the winged lion, later degraded by removal of the wings and then by insertion of a man's heart in place of a lion's heart of courage. A similar thing with respect to Israel can be found in Isaiah 3:1-8. Since this vision was given in the first year of Belshazzar, Daniel was being warned of the coming fall of Babylon, which came in his lifetime. Daniel had already had this vision when he was summoned to the drunken orgy related in Daniel 5. From this vision he knew what was coming.

The bear represents Persia. It is a very powerful but lumbering animal, lacking the speed of a lion or of the leopard which came third in the series. So history proved; Persia functioned like a steamroller (as Russia tried to do in World War 1 and did in World War 2) without the speed and agility of an Alexander the Great or of a modern Patton.

The leopard is already among the fastest of all animals, and with four wings its speed is emphasized. The reason for the four heads was that this conqueror's territory would be divided into four parts. So it was when Alexander the Great died that his generals divided the conquered territory into four parts. Military efforts to reunify the land were unsuccessful.

One point to note as to this vision is found in Revelation 13:2, where the final Anti-Christ will apparently have elements of the lion, bear and leopard. None of these kingdoms was godly at its core, although all of them did furnish enough order that some form of civilization could exist and God's people could live on from generation to generation. Militarily, one would expect the military and secret police of the Anti-Christ to combine the strength of the lion, the mass of the bear and the speed of the leopard. But this force and all other forces will be destroyed by the returning Jesus Christ. As Isaiah 2:4 says, *"He shall judge among many nations and shall rebuke many peoples. And they shall beat their swords into plowshares and their spears into pruning hooks. Nation shall not lift up sword against nation; neither shall they learn war any more."*

We should not imagine that the Lord Jesus in His resurrection body will assemble a more powerful military force from human sources when He returns. There is no need. Jesus Christ is in a new body that can move faster than any missile and indeed faster than light. His Word alone can and does kill (Revelation 19:15-21, see also 2 Thessalonians 2:8). The righteous angels, likewise more powerful than any human force and under His command, function as His police, jailors and courtroom bailiffs (Matthew 13:39-42, 25:31; Revelation 20:1-3). There is no extended campaign but rather a sudden and total destruction of the power of the Anti-Christ. Revelation 20 indicates that the final destruction of the Devil is postponed for a thousand years.

As in the first vision of Nebuchadnezzar, the fourth beast was iron. No animal was quite like it. The power and weight of this empire surpassed the others. But an additional element was revealed: the 10 horns which come out of that empire and the "little horn" (whom we will see again in chapter 11). I believe that the "little horn" has a double fulfillment: first as Antiochus Epiphanes, who profaned the Temple by sacrificing a sow on its altar, and then as the Anti-Christ who will demand that everyone (including the people of God—see 2 Thessalonians 2:3-4) worship him in the place of God Almighty.

There is both continuity and difference between the fourth empire of Rome and the kingdom of the Anti-Christ to come. The ten crowns and seven horns of Revelation 13:1 show the connection with Daniel 7, where the "little horn" uproots three kings and thus consolidates the conquered territory with his original place of authority. Historically, European law still looks to Roman law for its antecedents, not to English common law as we do in the United States. If someone speaks of the "Eternal City," we know that they speak of Rome even though we should also know that the heavenly Jerusalem of Revelation 21-22 is the only true eternal city. We can anticipate some form of analogy between ancient Rome and the wicked kingdom to come, but the parallels will not be exact.

Focusing on the little horn more closely, we find that he was a great orator, but of blasphemies instead of praises to God. (Daniel 7:8, 11:36; 2 Thessalonians 2:4, compare with Acts 12:21-23 for another forerunner; Matthew 24:11 for more forerunners; Revelation 13:1-6) He also lasts 42 months (Daniel 7:25, 12:7, Revelation 13:5—the parallel with Antiochus Ephiphanes is not exact as to time because from the blasphemous sacrifice of the pig to the cleansing of the Temple is 2300 days in Daniel 8:14). In addition, the "little horn" persecutes the people of God most intensely for his time in power (Daniel 7:21, 11:36; 2 Thessalonians 2:3-4, Revelation 13:4-7). He also demands and receives false worship (Daniel 11:36, 2 Thessalonians 2:3-4, Revelation 13:3-7). But when Jesus Christ comes he is thrown into the Lake of Fire and brimstone, never to emerge. Revelation 19:20.

The final image that Daniel 7 leaves is the triumph of Jesus Christ and of His saints of all ages. The rule of the Anti-Christ is 42 months, during which he runs rampant. But the rule of Jesus Christ and of His people is forever. <u>If we face tribulation for Christ's sake at any time, contrast the temporary nature of the trouble with the everlasting nature of the victory.</u>

Daniel 8 focuses most closely on the Persian and Greek periods. For us, one great purpose is to confirm the reliability of the Bible. The two-horned ram is Media-Persia, with the second horn Persia being the most prominent. The goat with the one horn was Greece under Alexander the Great. The Jews of the days of the war between Alexander and the Persian emperor Darius had no trouble recognizing the signs and avoided harm from the conflict.

Daniel 8 also gives us a picture of a "little horn" that is a forerunner of the Anti-Christ. This person desecrated the Temple by the sacrifice of a pig on its altar, a gross insult. From this rose the successful revolt of the Maccabees. In this case the Temple was cleansed after 2300 days. This cleansing is remembered today in December as Hanukkah.

CHAPTER 12 —
Daniel's Greatest Vision (Daniel 9)

By this time Daniel was past normal retirement age. Surprisingly, Daniel's most significant vision was yet to come. Like so many blessings from God, this one started with Bible study. Daniel was reading Jeremiah (25:11-12, 29:10) when he discovered that God had set the time of exile at 70 years. Daniel realized that he himself had been in captivity (Daniel's circumstances were relatively comfortable compared to many, but he was nevertheless a captive) for 70 years himself. This jolted Daniel into a storm of prayer. We know from his earlier history that Daniel was a man of regular prayer. This prayer in Daniel 9 is one of the most fervent in all of Scripture short of the prayers of our Lord Jesus (especially John 17 for comparison). Daniel was praying for the restoration of God's people to the land promised them by God to Abraham, Isaac and Jacob and repeated to David.

One great principle of Daniel's prayer is that he approached God with humility with recognition of his own sin and the sin of his people for whom he was praying. There was no claim of any right to God's blessing. The only basis of blessing is the mercy of God, not anything about us. The tax collector, not the Pharisee, was like Daniel in this respect (Luke 18:10-14). Daniel was one of the holiest of men short of the Lord Jesus Himself (see Ezekiel 14:14-20). In that very holiness Daniel saw his uncleanness compared to God Himself.

A second great principle is that Daniel had no doubt about the power to God to perform His promises. Daniel had seen great miracles, but his faith predated the miracles that he witnessed, as we saw in the discussion of Daniel's approach as a young men to be permitted to eat according to Mosaic law.

In this case Daniel prayed with fasting and personal discomfort. There is no indication that this was a ritual fast or a scheduled fast, but rather Daniel fasted and displayed sackcloth and ashes as a physical representation of deep repentance (compare Job 42:6 and Jonah 3:4-10). There may be times in our lives when it is appropriate to fast, although we have no scheduled fasts because the Holy Spirit is ever with us and we already are connected with the Bridegroom. There remains a time for mourning and even for fasting, but the predominant notes in the Christian life should be peace and joy in the Holy Spirit. For Daniel, this was a time of fasting and intense spiritual warfare as part of the battle to restore Israel to the Holy Land.

Some interpreters have stated that every Jew who remained in formerly Babylonian territory was violating the command of God. I think that is too sweeping a generalization. Daniel himself had no reason to return and every reason to remain. He was probably too old to keep up with a caravan across desert terrain. As a eunuch, Daniel could never have worshiped in a restored Temple (in fact, the Temple would not be completed for another 20 years, but that probably was not yet known). As one of the three presidents over the provincial satraps or even as the head over those three presidents, Daniel was in a far better position to help the Jewish people at the seat of the Persian government than he ever could have in Jerusalem. Later history would prove that Jewish representation was still required at the seat of Persian government long after the first wave returned to Judea. The history of Nehemiah and of Mordecai and Esther is sufficient proof of this. There is probably just criticism that more younger people who were strong enough to withstand pioneer rigors and without binding ties in Babylon did not return. But even Abraham remained at Nahor until his father had died and so gave due regard to the responsibilities of a son to an aged and infirm father. Some Jews in Babylon probably faced a similar situation. Daniel himself remained where God had placed him.

The angel told Daniel that he was "greatly beloved" by God (Daniel 9:23). What an honor! Daniel's humble spirit was a part of this. Daniel was diligent in studying the Scriptures that were available to him. We, who have the complete Bible, bear a greater responsibility to likewise study God's Word. Daniel was a man of fervent prayer; by this time Daniel had had a whole lifetime of answered prayer. We may not have Daniel's experience in prayer, but we must strive to improve in prayer just as a diligent quarterback like Tim Tebow strives to improve his football. Prayer does not take physical strength nor even age. Even a child with a brand-new faith can begin. Prayer does take faith and perseverance (for example, Luke 18:1-8), but not necessarily a great intellect like Daniel or Paul. *The effective, fervent prayer of a righteous man avails much.* James 5:16.

Daniel's prayer was indeed heard favorably by God as within His revealed will in prophetic Scripture. In fact the answer went beyond the prayer to reveal a timetable for the Messiah, although this was not apparent immediately. I believe that Daniel 9:24-27, like Isaiah 7:14 and many other prophetic passages, has two (or in a few cases more than two) layers of truth. I realize that some expositors believe that there is but one true interpretation of any verse in the Bible. I would agree that contradictory interpretations cannot both be true, but multiple interpretations may simultaneously be true if they are not contradictory to one another and do not violate the rest of Scripture taken as a whole. To take a simple example, I believe that Isaiah 7:14 refers to two distinct births in one prophecy: (1) A short-range prophecy of the birth of an heir to King Ahaz's throne; and (2) A long-range prophecy of the birth of Jesus the Messiah. The Septuagint translators about 270 BC were in agreement with my dual-prophecy view, translating a Hebrew word that means a "young woman" who may or may not be a virgin in Greek to a word that specifically means a virgin, emphasizing the birth yet future to them as the primary thrust of the prophecy. Matthew followed the Septuagint translators.

For convenience I will set out Daniel 9:24-27 so that one can follow the argument for a dual meaning of the prophecy given to Daniel:

Seventy weeks are determined upon your people [the people of Israel] and upon your holy city [Jerusalem) to

(1) To finish the transgression
(2) And make an end of sins
(3) And to make reconciliation for iniquity
(4) And to bring in everlasting righteousness
(5) And to seal up the vision and prophecy
(6) And to anoint (or "to messiah") the Most Holy.

Know therefore and understand that from the going forth of the commandment to restore and build Jerusalem until Messiah the Prince shall be seven weeks and sixty-two weeks. The street and the wall shall be built again in troubled times.

And after sixty-two weeks Messiah shall be cut off, but not for Himself. And the people of the prince that shall come shall destroy the city and the sanctuary, and the end of it shall be with a flood, and until the end of the war desolations are determined.

And he (or He) shall confirm the covenant with many for one week, and in the middle of the week, and in the middle of the week he (or He) shall cause the sacrifice and the oblation to cease, and for the overspreading of abominations he (or He) shall make it desolate, even until the consummation, and that determined shall be poured on the desolate.

As a preliminary matter, almost all commentators agree that the "weeks" in this case are seven-year periods rather than our usual 7-day periods, as they were in the case of Jacob working for his wives (Genesis 29:27). So the 69 weeks total 483 years (leaving aside the question of whether God was speaking of our solar calendar or of the lunar calendar laid out by Moses). From our backward look at the history, we know that Nehemiah records a later confirmation of Cyrus' decree permitting the reconstruction of Jerusalem. If one goes forward 483 years from there, one arrives at the beginning of the ministry of Jesus Christ. I cannot be precise because of the precise dates of the birth of Christ and of the start of His ministry is unknown, although most agree that the original dating of the birth of Christ was off by several years. Accordingly, God has likewise concealed the precise time of the Second Coming as well. However, many do agree that from the very beginning of His ministry to His death and resurrection is a period of 3½ years, the equivalent of 42 months.

Having laid out the elements of the prophecy, let us test a dual interpretation by the rest of the Holy Scriptures. I will proceed in order of time of my dual interpretations. Since I believe that this prophecy applies to both the first and second comings of Jesus the Messiah, I will test my theory first as applied to His life in human flesh and then as applied to His Return to earth from heaven. If you feel the need to study further the Virgin Birth, then Matthew 1 and Luke 1-3 would be the places to go. As for the Second Coming, the promise of the angel in Acts 1:11 is a good starting point, along with 1 Thessalonians 4:13-18 and 2 Thessalonians 1:7-10.

FIRST COMING

Did the Lord Jesus "finish the transgression" when He served on the earth? He certainly did bring all transgression to a head. Never was there such a monstrous injustice as the execution of Jesus Christ after He was found by Judge Pilate as without fault three times. Isaiah 53 and 1 Peter 2:24 certainly indicate that He paid the price of sin in full. If we understand by this that the Lord Jesus destroyed beyond repair Satan's kingdom over the nations, Jesus Christ did this too (Colossians 2:15, Ephesians 1:20-22).

Did Jesus Christ "make an end of sins" at the Cross? Certainly! Romans 4 is the most extended treatment of this topic, teaching that

He paid the complete penalty for all the sin of His people. Colossians 2:14 shows that He legally (though not as a moral guide) erased the Law that accuses us of sin. Romans 4:15 agrees, teaching that *"Where there is no law, there is no transgression."* Our American Constitution recognizes this principle in its <u>ex poste facto</u> clause. However disgusting some conduct may be, there can be no legal punishment if there is no law making the conduct criminal when the act was performed and prescribing punishment. That is why Cain did not face an immediate death sentence for murdering Abel. For His people, our Lord Jesus has done exactly this: He has wiped out the Law of God in the aspect that it accuses us of sin against God and therefore declares us worthy of immediate death. One reason that our transgressions are forgiven is that the Law of God is erased as an accusation. Since there is no longer a charge against us, there can no longer be a trial or a guilty verdict. However, this is true only of those who repent of their sinful nature and their sins in particular and trust Jesus Christ as Lord and Savior. The erasure of God's Law as an accuser does not apply to all people. Revelation 20 and 2 Thessalonians 1 & 2 are portions of the New Testament that make this clear.

Further, Jesus Christ blotted out our sins as well as blotting out the Law as an accusing document. He *"bore our sins in His own body on the tree."* 1 Peter 2:24. *As far as the east is from the west, so far has He removed our transgressions from us.* Psalm 103:12. King David's prayer was answered and is answered for all of His people: *"Hide Your face from my sins, and blot out all my iniquities."* Psalm 51:9. Asaph prayed, *"Do not remember against us former iniquities; let your tender mercies go before us, for we are brought very low."* Psalm 79:8. Job testifies also, *"My transgression is sealed up in a bag, and You sew up my iniquity."* Job 14:17. Colossians 2:13-14 deals with both aspects: our transgressions are forgiven and the Law has been erased.

Did Jesus Christ "make reconciliation for iniquity" during His life on earth? The New Testament clearly says yes. Romans 5:10 instructs us that Christ died for us while we were still His enemies. In addition,

He reconciled us to His Father, overcoming the enmity. 2 Corinthians 5:18-21 deals with Christ's reconciliation of us to the Father and also of the world as a whole to the Father. Clearly not every human being will be reconciled and saved, and just as clearly there will be a new heavens and a new earth (Revelation 21-22) to replace this fallen universe (Romans 8:18-22). Colossians 1:21-22 treats salvation and reconciliation together. So it is clear that the life of Jesus Christ on earth satisfied this portion of Daniel's prophecy.

Did Jesus Christ "bring in everlasting righteousness" by His work on earth? To answer this question, let us refer back to Daniel's original vision in chapter 2 in which the "stone made without hands" smashed to bits the image of the four empires (Daniel 2:44). The kingdom from that stone shall never be destroyed. That kingdom, which is the Kingdom of God, may be attacked daily for the time being but it will never be conquered. It has not yet been destroyed almost 2000 years after the Resurrection, even though it has been under attack during that entire period. Neither Hitler, nor Stalin, nor Mao were able to destroy the Christian church within their respective countries. There are still Christians in North Korea today after decades of near-starvation. The entire thrust of Revelation is that the Kingdom of God, with Jesus the Messiah as equal co-regent with His Father, destroys Satan and his kingdom forever rather than the other way around. Consider the closing of the Lord's Prayer: *"For Yours is the Kingdom, and the power, and the glory forever and ever. Amen."*

Did Jesus Christ "seal up the vision and prophecy" through His life on earth? This answer is clear enough in that Revelation is the last book of the Bible and that all of the books of the Bible were complete before the departure of the last apostle who knew Jesus as the Son of Man in His Virgin-born body. Adding another book behind Revelation is inconceivable. In fact there is a severe warning against adding to Revelation in Revelation 22:18.

Was Jesus Christ anointed (or "messiahed") as the Most Holy on earth? Psalm 45, portraying Jesus as Messiah and King, gives a clear answer. As a counterpart, Hebrews 1:3 portrays the risen Jesus the Messiah as being seated at God's right hand. This is not only the place of honor; it is also the place of equality because nobody inferior can sit in the presence of the Sovereign absent special permission. Philippians 2:5-11 ties into this, showing that *"at the name of Jesus every knee shall bow . . ."* (v. 10) Hitler will bow; Stalin will bow; Mao will bow. So will all the famous atheists like Robert Ingersoll and Carl Sagan. So will the judges of the Sanhedrin that condemned Jesus to death, and so will all the persecutors such as Ahab, Jezebel and Haman. All these and billions more will bow in abject terror with good reason.

Going beyond His kingship, the Lord Jesus was also the High Priest of the order of Melchizedek, as prophesied in Psalm 110 and introduced in Hebrews 6:20 and amplified in Hebrews 7-8. Romans 8:34 specifies that our Lord Jesus intercedes for us as He did for Peter long ago.

As for prophecy, Matthew 24, Mark 13 and Luke 21 are sufficient examples to prove Jesus' credentials as an anointed prophet of His Father. The very night of His arrest, Jesus predicted accurately Peter's denials. He also predicted the coming of the Holy Spirit in John 16:7-10. There are many other examples, but these are sufficient to show Jesus as a prophet. Thus, the Lord Jesus fulfilled perfectly all of the anointed offices of the Old Testament and was therefore anointed as the Most Holy. He was to be equally the subject of worship with His Father. (John 5:19-30)

Does the 70th week have any application to the our Lord's life on earth? I would suggest that the revelation that "He shall confirm a covenant with many for one week" and that "He shall break the covenant in the middle of the week" has a fulfillment with respect to the first coming of Jesus Christ in human flesh. The Sermon on the Mount came early in our Lord's ministry. He said, *"I came not to destroy [the Law], but to fulfill."* Matthew 5:17. This is one example of His confirmation of the existing covenant. Time and again our Lord Jesus referred to the Old Testament as binding. Another example is His answer to the rich young ruler in Luke 18:20, referring to the second half of the Ten Commandments. At first our Lord did not mention the Tenth Commandment—*You shall not covet.* But the rich young ruler professed to fulfill those Commandments that our Lord mentioned at first. Then the Lord Jesus pressed home the Tenth Commandment by pressing the rich young ruler to sell everything he had. The Lord Jesus' dealing with the rich young ruler is another example of His confirmation of the Covenant.

The total duration of the ministry of the Lord Jesus Christ appears to have been 3½ years, which would match one-half of one week of years. What happened at the Cross, at the end of the 3½ years? We know that the Old Covenant was fulfilled completely as to the sacrificial requirement to pay for our sin, but we also know that the Old Covenant was broken, never to be revived again in its original form. The first sign was the rending of the Temple veil (Matthew 27:51). The Shekinah glory was no longer behind the veil, so the veil itself became useless. No longer would God be approached through animal sacrifices, which had existed ever since an animal was killed to provide a covering for Adam and Eve. In some form animal sacrifices long predate Moses' Law, as shown in the lives of Abraham and Job. But all of that is now finished. Jeremiah 30-33 and Ezekiel 36 predicted a New Covenant. The Book of Hebrews (chapter 7-8 and especially 8:13) makes it clear that Jesus Christ set aside the Old Covenant in order to establish the New Covenant in its place. Part of this change is the elimination of the old priesthood in favor of the entire Body of Christ as a holy nation and a royal priesthood (1 Peter 2:9). Another part is the elimination of the spiritual distinction between Jew and Gentile first clearly decided in Acts 15 and taught at length by the Apostle Paul in Galatians 3 (especially 3:28-29) and in Ephesians 2:11-22. Romans 2:28-29 points to this too. Still another is the elimination of many ordinances that were observed under the Old Covenant. (Hebrews 9 is the most extended treatment of this.) Under the New Covenant baptism and the Lord's Table are the only universally required sacraments according to the Scriptures. This is only a quick sketch of the differences between the Old and New Covenants, but this should be sufficient to establish that the Lord Jesus did break the Old Covenant "in the middle of the week."

Where is the second half of the 70th week under this fulfillment? The answer lies in the fulfillment of the warnings of Jesus Christ recorded in Matthew 24, Mark 13 and Luke 21 of the destruction of the Temple, of Jerusalem and of Israel. The precise history of the prophesied destruction is not found in the Scriptures but is well known to us through the testimony of Josephus and of other Roman historians. The evidence of that destruction endures to this day in the form of the Wailing Wall. I would posit that only the Nazis or the Mongols of all the destroyers of history come close to the thoroughness of the destruction of the Temple and of Jerusalem. Not even the entire cities of Hiroshima and Nagasaki were as thoroughly destroyed as Jerusalem by the cumulative effect of the 3½ year revolt and ended by a terrible siege and by crushing, fiery defeat. The thoroughness of the destruction also answers to the destructive thoroughness of Daniel's Fourth Beast in his vision of Daniel 7.

ANALYSIS OF DANIEL 9:24-27 WITH RESPECT TO THE SECOND COMING

The term "finish the transgression" has clear application to the Second Coming as well as to the First Coming. If our Lord Jesus made the end of transgression certain by His death on the Cross and His resurrection from the tomb, He will finish off the remaining resistance of sin at His Second Coming. The armies that Satan has gathered at Armageddon are slaughtered at His command. Revelation 19:20-21; Isaiah 11:4. Just as the universe and life came into existence at God's command, so the armies of the wicked are killed at Jesus' command at His return. The Beast and False Prophet are taken alive and thrown into the Lake of Fire ahead of the rest of the wicked. They will follow when the Lord Jesus gives the command (Matthew 25:31-46).

The same comments apply to the Second Coming as related to "make an end of sins." Revelation 21-22 explains in detail the absence of sin in the new heavens and the new earth. The rituals of the Law of Moses pointed toward complete purification of the believer in the presence of God. The new body taught in 1 Corinthians 15 likewise is necessary for the complete absence of sin in the new heavens and the new earth. Peter in 2 Peter 3:13 predicts a new earth where righteousness lives, unlike this present earth which is in bondage to death and where righteousness is hard to find. That entire chapter connects the requirement for holiness in our current lives with the absolute holiness of the next life. In this sense we are all engaged in rehearsals for our new lives in our new bodies. As any musician knows, we must sing well in practice in order to sing our best in performance. Beyond that, we need grace from God which we have not yet experienced. But indeed our Lord Jesus will "make an end of sins when He returns." (As to exact sequence and timing, we will bypass the issue of the Millenium for the sake of clarity in understanding Daniel's prophecy.)

Both of the previous paragraphs apply to "make reconciliation for iniquity" as well. Not even John the Baptist, the greatest of all men born of woman, was worthy even to untie Jesus' sandal. (John 1:27) And yet Jesus' disciples were raised from servants (for example, John 15:20) to friends (John 15:13-15, compare James 2:23) to brothers (Romans 8:17, 29). It is astounding and beyond comprehension to think that God Almighty would raise me from a wretched rebel fully worthy of eternal damnation and torment to a brother of His Anointed Son Jesus Christ by sacrificing that Anointed Son, but that is what God has done. None of us can be thankful enough. In my case, my own mind and emotions are so numb when I try to meditate on this that I hardly respond at all compared to the humble thanks that would begin to be appropriate. And yet I have been given the Holy Spirit as the down payment of the promised gift of an eternal place with Jesus Christ in the eternal Kingdom of God to come (Ephesians 1:13-14).

Much of the same can be said for the relationship between "bring in everlasting righteousness" and the Second Coming. We can go back to the familiar close of the Lord's Prayer: *"For Yours is the kingdom, and the power and the glory forever. Amen."* Consider also Hebrews 12:27, which distinguishes between those things now existing which can be shaken from those that cannot be shaken. Revelation 16:18-20 and Isaiah 24 speak of that last terrible earthquake which shakes the entire earth. Spiritually there will be a parallel shaking answering to the physical one portrayed there, as shown by the purifying judgment fire for believers of 1 Corinthians 3:11-15 and 1 Peter 1:7. In this way everlasting righteousness will grow from a hope to a fact and a reality.

If during His first coming the Lord Jesus "sealed up the vision and prophecy" by His works and by sending the Holy Spirit to His disciples and other believers of that generation who completed the Holy Scriptures, then His Second Coming will bring all yet unfulfilled or partially fulfilled prophecies to full fruition and fact. In "destroying the works of the Devil" (1 John 3:8), Jesus will also reverse all of the damage done by the fall of Satan and the fall of Adam and Eve. Revelation 22 makes this clear. There will be no weeping, no death, no pain and no grief. As Isaiah said, *"Therefore the redeemed of the Lord shall return and come with singing to Zion and everlasting joy shall be on their heads. They shall obtain gladness and joy, and sorrow and mourning shall flee away."* Isaiah 51:11. We cannot yet understand what all of this will be like, but it is coming because God has promised.

Jesus already became the Messiah at His First Coming. Yet Psalm 45:6-7 connects His reign as King with His anointing. At present He is seated at God's right hand and reigns with His Father (Hebrews 1) but the time has not yet come for Jesus to exercise His full dictatorial powers as illustrated in Matthew 25:31-46. Both 1 Corinthians 15:25-28 and Hebrews 2:8 speak of everything in principle being under the feet of Jesus, but we know that not all things are in subjection to Him yet. The anointing of Jesus as King has a fulfillment which yet remains and which applies to His Second Coming. When this is fulfilled, the Lord Jesus will be Lord of All and will function as subject to His Father and yet fully equal with Him in a way that we do not yet fully understand.

I am somewhat unusual in believing that Daniel's 70th week has two fulfillments, one of which was completed by the Roman destruction of the Temple and of Jerusalem. The more conventional view reserves the 70th week entirely to the 2nd coming, and I do agree that there is a coming fulfillment of the 70th week just before the Second Coming. As background, we should remember that the Anti-Christ does his best to counterfeit the genuine Jesus Christ. Satan does his best to counterfeit God and genuine miracles. Our Lord Jesus warned of such false miracles in Matthew 24: 11, 23-27. In fact, Satan counterfeits the Trinity itself, forming a *troika* with the Anti-Christ (or the Beast) and the False Prophet. And so the Anti-Christ will try to imitate the fulfillment by Jesus Christ of Daniel's 70th week. Like a judo grandmaster, God will let this false front proceed so far as part of His second and final fulfillment of Daniel's prophecy and then destroy the entire *troika*.

Is the Anti-Christ yet alive on the earth? We do not know, but it is reasonable to suspect that he is already alive although he has not been unmasked. In fact, the Anti-Christ during his earlier years may not know that he is the Anti-Christ, just as Hitler as a bohemian artist in Vienna had no ambition to be the dictator of Germany. When he begins his rise to world power, we would expect the Anti-Christ to uproot three other small kingdoms based on Daniel 7:24 and then to negotiate a 7-year treaty with Israel. We would reasonably anticipate that when the Anti-Christ breaks this covenant in the "middle of the week," he will likewise demand worship in the spiritual Temple of Christ's body (2 Thessalonians 2:4) and also in the Jewish Temple if in fact one has been rebuilt. Revelation 13 gives another view of this last half of the 70th week, which corresponds spiritually in the outward persecution of the Church to the earlier destruction of national Israel as shown by the double fulfillment of Matthew 24 (Mark 13 and Luke

21 cover the same teaching, although they seem to emphasize more the first fulfillment of the destruction than does Matthew 24). I expect the Anti-Christ to hate and attack both national Israel and the Church. Clearly the 70th week of Daniel is connected to the Second Coming of the Lord Jesus.

QUESTIONS FOR REFLECTION AND DISCUSSION

1. Are we prepared to suffer if necessary for the name of the Lord Jesus Christ?
2. To what extent are our hopes bound up with earthly objects that are reserved for destruction (2 Peter 3:7)?
3. How strong is our relationship to Jesus Christ compared to our relationships with our family and friends who may removed from us at any time (Matthew 19:29, Luke 14:26)?
4. Daniel was "greatly beloved" by God. Do we have enough sense of the Lord Jesus so that He is our beloved (even beyond our spouses for those of us who are married)? We may know Him as real, but do we also feel Him as real without discarding our knowledge which is also necessary?

CHAPTER 13 —
DANIEL 10 AND BEYOND

Daniel 10 introduces another vision with specific application to the period of Greek dominance over the Holy Land, with one of those Greek-cultured rulers being a forerunner of the Anti-Christ. All of this was part of the detailed road-map that God was giving the Jewish people to guide them to the Messiah and the time of His first appearance on earth. But before we peek at this, we are given a rare glimpse into an invisible spiritual world which has hidden influence upon the physical world of time and space in which we now live. We are never permitted to attempt to communicate directly into that spiritual world; the Christian's communication is with the Father through the sacrifice of His Son and with the Holy Spirit within. That is more than enough for us because God himself is in control of the spirit world despite Satan's pretensions and continued efforts to foment a rebellion.

As an aside, since this prophecy is of a time of Greek culture and religious influence, we should observe that in the Greek myths Zeus and his allies overthrew the original gods, the Titans. In a broad sense one can reasonably argue that Greek mythology in its religious aspects imagines what might have happened if Satan had actually overthrown God Himself. Of course Satan's rebellion failed, although one-third of the angels (inferred from the one-third of the stars of heaven having fallen in Revelation 12:4) and the majority of humanity have joined his rebellion. Satan's rebellion is well on its way to Ronald Reagan's "dustbin of history", although ash-heap might be a better description considering that all the rebels who do not repent end up in perpetual torment in the Lake of Fire. But until the suppression of the rebellion is complete, there is the hidden conflict in the spiritual world between the forces of Satan and the forces of God.

During the first half of the 20th century one finds it hard to imagine two more Satanic political regimes that Nazi Germany and Soviet Russia. Hitler and Stalin are two of the cruelest men ever to lead major nations. I believe that their spiritual master Satan decided to crash them into each other just to see how much destruction and misery he could cause, for the fleeting delight of the pyromaniac. God permitted all this for His own purposes. This illustrates the tremendous truth of what Jesus Christ said in Matthew 12:25: *"Every kingdom divided against itself is brought to desolation, and every city or house divided against itself shall not stand."* The next two verses show that Satan's kingdom is divided against itself and therefore cannot stand. So it was in the times of Daniel's visions with the coming conflicts among the successive kingdoms portrayed and so it will be at the very end when the nations are prepared to fight a battle of extermination at Armageddon. Satan's kingdom may cause terrible destruction for a time, but it will fall forever.

For other glimpses in the Bible of portions of this spirit world, look at 2 Kings 6:16-18 and Luke 22:43.

In the immediate context of Daniel 10, Daniel was in the crossfire between demons exercising influence over Persia and angels communicating understanding of the vision to Daniel. The short-run effect was that Daniel was physically sick and unable to eat for 3 weeks. Just as in physical battle, being present at the epicenter of a conflict will bring extraordinary stress. The grace of God is sufficient to overcome that stress, but the stress will exist nevertheless. 1 Corinthians 10:13. The life of victory in Jesus Christ is not a life free of conflict or pain but a life of triumph in conflict and triumph despite pain.

QUESTION FOR REFLECTION OR DISCUSSION

Do you feel or have you felt like a soccer ball, being kicked at from every direction? If so, have you acted or spoken in a way to trigger your situation, as did Samson and David? Or have others placed you in the cross-hairs without a good reason (Psalm 35:7, 69:4, 119:78,161)?

If you are a Christian, Satan will target you for that reason alone (1 Peter 5:8). The Holy Spirit through Peter instructed us to "watch unto prayer (1 Peter 4:7)." Compare Mark 13:33-37, Luke 21:36. Do you figuratively wear your spiritual armor described in Ephesians 6:10-18 to be prepared against a surprise attack by Satan?

Most of Daniel 11 is the history of the conflict among the Greek-cultured states that arose in the wake of the death of Alexander the Great. This was essential information for the leaders of the Jews, lest they get caught on the wrong side of a war without an army of their own. Today the preliminary stages are interesting primarily to historians and I will therefore spend little time on this. Since Daniel's prophecy is centered on Israel as a people and on the Holy Land, the focus is on the conflict between the Ptolemy dynasty based in Egypt and the Seleucid dynasty based in Syria, because it was these two states that contested the Holy Land. Originally, the Ptolemies ruled it, somewhat as the Pharaohs had often done before Moses. But the Seleucids succeeded in ousting them shortly after 200 BC. In another generation there was a drastic change in the religious toleration afforded the Jewish people under the Persians (Haman aside) and under the early Greek rulers.

But Daniel 11:21 introduces a "vile person" who merits our attention. This person in verse 23 breaks an alliance, which sounds similar to the actions of the Anti-Christ described in Daniel 9:24-27 in breaking a covenant. Since the time dimension for the "vile person" does not match the Anti-Christ, it is right and reasonable to believe that the "vile person" of Daniel 11:21 is a forerunner of the Anti-Christ and spiritually similar in an analogous manner that King David was a forerunner of Jesus the Messiah, the King of Israel. Although it was not obvious in Jonah's lifetime, Jonah was also a forerunner of Jesus Christ in his confinement for 3 days and 3 nights in the belly of the great fish, as the Lord Jesus was 3 days and 3 nights in the Tomb after His crucifixion. The "vile person" not only broke an alliance but also desecrated the Temple (compare 2 Thessalonians 2:4 and the "abomination of desolation" mentioned by the Lord Jesus in Matthew 24:15, referring in my view to the original occurrence prophesied in Daniel 11:36 and probably also referring to Daniel 9:27 as applied to the Anti-Christ).

History fills in the details that the Scriptures themselves do not record. The Books of the Maccabees are not fully inspired scriptures but they are reasonably reliable history. The same is true of the writings of Josephus, the Jewish historian who lived through the destruction of Israel by the Romans. Roughly 160 to 170 years before the birth of Jesus Christ, the Seleucid ruler Antiochus Epiphanes (indicating that he was somewhat insane) lost a military campaign against the Ptolemies of Egypt. On his retreat to Jerusalem, he revoked the toleration of the Jews and desecrated the Temple by sacrificing a sow on the Temple altar, a deliberate sacrilege. This in turn provoked the Maccabees to a revolution, which ultimately was successful enough to secure a precarious independence for a small buffer Jewish state between the Seleucids and the Ptolemies. When the Temple was cleansed of the sacrilege after the 2300 days given to Daniel (8:14), there was an extreme shortage of oil for the lamps of the Temple. The miracle of Hanukkah is that the oil did not run out before another consecrated supply became available at the time of restoration of worship at the Temple. I am prepared to believe that the miracle occurred based on ancient historical testimony, but I would also state that this miracle is overshadowed by the Virgin Birth, death, burial and resurrection of Jesus the Messiah.

Josephus gives eyewitness testimony to the destruction of the Temple in 70 AD, about 40 years after the death of our Lord Jesus Christ and perhaps 3 years after the executions of Peter and Paul. As the Lord Jesus warned in Matthew 24:2, no stones were left standing of the Temple. From the photos I see of the Wailing Wall, even this looks like a foundation wall to my eye, although I am not an archeologist. The Temple was not only desecrated this time but razed to the ground. The fire was so hot that the soldiers broke the stones apart to get at the molten gold to supplement their pay. This was the climax of the Jewish War that raged for 3½ years, as indicated in Daniel 9 and also in Daniel 12:7, matched in the time period given in Revelation 13:5.

My conclusion is that the desecration of Antiochus Epiphanes, the destruction of the Temple by the Romans and the reign of the Anti-Christ at the end of the age are spiritually linked and that understanding the earlier outrages will shed light on the future of the Anti-Christ. All three men (two long dead and one yet to be revealed) are great destroyers. In each case the wicked ruler targets the worship of God and persecutes those who worship Him instead of the human ruler, like North Korea today. For this, note the similarity between Daniel 11:36-42 and Revelation 13. I am inclined to believe that part of Daniel 11:36-45 has not yet been fulfilled in full but will be fulfilled by the Anti-Christ, who is a magnification of the false principles and wicked character of Antiochus Epiphanes.

We should amplify the point that one of Satan's goals is to persuade a person to worship himself or herself, assuming that the person will not worship Satan directly. Albert Speer during his imprisonment came to see that fundamentally Adolf Hitler worshiped himself, as he wrote in his book *Inside the Third Reich*. An example from the Bible is found in Acts 12:20-23 when one of the rulers named Herod (not the original Herod that slaughtered the baby boys of Bethlehem) received a flattering oration as if he were a god. The response of the true God was swift and decisive: the pretender Herod became worm-eaten in his intestines and died in agony. Haman showed the same sin when he imagined that the king must be intending to honor him (Esther 6:6-10). The five "I will" statements of Satan in Isaiah 14:13-14 show Satan's abandonment to self-worship. In contrast Job, having heard God, said that "I abhor myself and repent in dust and ashes."

Job 42:6. The Apostle Paul counted himself the chief of sinners (1 Timothy 1:15). The sinless Lord Jesus "humbled Himself and became obedient to death, even to the death of the Cross." (Philippians 2:8) Our worship of Christ Jesus and our humbling of ourselves go hand in hand. Satan's attitude, expressed in Daniel 11:36-42 and elsewhere, is to exalt self and rebel against God. In contrast, the kings who sought out the Messiah not only acknowledged the truth of His Deity but also humbled themselves in worship as they gave their gifts even though the Messiah that they worshiped was an apparently helpless baby to bare human sight.

QUESTION FOR REFLECTION AND DISCUSSION

If we were to live into the times of the Anti-Christ, are we prepared to "obey God rather than men" (Acts 4:19-20. 5:29) regardless of the earthly consequences? Do we believe the promise of Matthew 19:28-30?

CHAPTER 14 —
NOTES ON DANIEL 12

We should remember that the chapter and verse divisions were not in the original Scriptures but were added in medieval times to permit faster reference to particular portions of the text. Having said that, I do believe that the start of a new chapter as Daniel 12 is right. This portion appears to be a synopsis of the end of days. Daniel was promised that his people—Israel—would be delivered, with the qualifying phrase that those delivered must be "written in the Book." This appears again in Revelation 20:11-15. I believe that Romans 11:25-32 indicates that every child of Jacob (renamed Israel) living at the return of Messiah is among those written in the Book of Life and redeemed, but that particular issue can be reserved for closer examination without losing the flow of Daniel 12. For my own views, I would refer the reader to chapter 8 of my previous book Fight to the Finish, published by Trafford Press,

Have you ever been told that the Old Testament does not teach the resurrection of the dead? Bunk! Daniel 12:2 could not be clearer, but even in the Old Testament it does not stand alone. Job 14:10-17 and Job 19:23-27 show that the ancients knew of the the resurrection of the dead. Job was composed long before Moses received the Law. Just as Paul argued in Galatians 3:17 that the Law could not repeal the covenant already made for Abraham in Christ, so I would add as a corollary that the Law could not repeal the promises of resurrection already of record in Job. Later comes Psalm 16. These are not the only passages in the Old Testament to speak of resurrection, but they are sufficient to establish the resurrection of the dead as Old Testament doctrine. So Daniel makes more explicit previous teaching in Daniel 12:2 rather than introducing something totally new.

Daniel also makes clear that not all people who shall be raised from the dead shall will enjoy blessing from God. He expresses the dichotomy as "everlasting life" as opposed to "everlasting shame and contempt." It is true that the New Testament is more explicit both as to joys of everlasting life and of the horrors of everlasting shame and contempt, but the New Testament and particularly the teaching both of Jesus Christ on earth and Revelation rest on a foundation sketched by Daniel. Proverbs 10:7 hints at life after death: *The memory of the just is blessed, but the name of the wicked shall rot.* If there is no life after death, what does this matter (as indeed Paul argued in 1 Corinthians 15:32)? Adolf Hitler has no reason to care that his name is hated over the whole world if he is not facing the judgment of God. But as matters truly are, he and many others have every reason to dread the Last Judgment and their perpetual torments that they face. The Gospel of Matthew and Revelation are especially detailed in unfolding the Last Judgment (for example, Matthew 25:31-46 and Revelation 20:11-15).

Daniel also mentions the importance of witnessing to the Gospel. Daniel 12:3 reflects Proverbs 11:30. As Isaiah also said before Daniel, *"How beautiful upon the mountains are the feet of him that brings good tidings, that publishes peace, that brings good tidings of good, that publishes salvation, that says to Zion, 'Your God reigns!'"* Isaiah 52:7. Our Lord Jesus identified one of the indications of the coming end as the gospel being preached to all nations. Matthew 24:14.

Daniel 12:4 gives two more signs which would appear near the end of the age. *"Men shall run to and fro, and knowledge shall increase."* The increase in travel over the last 4 centuries is obvious. When English colonists and refugees first came to American shores, it took several months to cross the Atlantic. By the time of the *Titanic* about 3 centuries later, that time had been reduced to several days. On land, railroads had just about eliminated the horse and carriage for intercity transport at probably double the speed. Now automobile travel vastly exceeds the speed of railroads except for special high speed rail. In the meantime the airplane is faster than even high-speed rail. It used to be common for people to be born, grow in, marry in, work in and die in the same town or village. Now people travel across the world as a matter of routine, even for vacations. Both the speed and the amount of travel has increased vastly in recent history.

As for knowledge, computer storage has made the distribution of information much faster and easier. We may not have a precise measure of the number of known facts nor the importance of each, but it is apparent from the rise of data mining that the amount of information has increased vastly and that the use of computers is enabling new uses and analyses of the information that is available. In my lifetime we have gone from the Univac, then mainframe computers to desktop and laptop computers that leave the best of the old computers in the dust. To take my own computer history as an example, my first computer was a Xerox 820 with dual floppy disks of 64K each; programs had overlay files to accommodate the tiny memory of the computer. The first hard drives were 5 megabytes; I started with a Kaypro 10 with 10 megabytes of storage. Now we discuss terabytes in storage and gigabytes of RAM. One could trace parallel developments in genomic knowledge, in medicine and in numerous other subjects. Like the travel increase, the increase in human knowledge, while capable of wonderful applications, is a warning that the end of days is drawing close. How close? I cannot say with precision. But Daniel 12:7 does say that the Anti-Christ will ride roughshod over the "holy people" for 3½ years just before the finish of history as we now know it.

When Daniel wanted to inquire further (in verses 12:8 and following), God stopped him and gently told Daniel to stick to what God had chosen to reveal to him. We still have to accept God's refusal to Daniel, even with the additional information that we have received in the New Testament. Jesus Himself did not know the day nor the hour of His return, and we cannot know either. But we are commanded in many places to watch and be ready. The time may be sooner than we expect.

APPENDIX A — FUNDAMENTAL DIFFERENCES BETWEEN CHRISTIAN AND MUSLIM CONCEPTS OF THE SECOND COMING OF OUR LORD JESUS CHRIST

Undoubtedly there is some variation among Muslims about their exact doctrine of the return of the Lord Jesus Christ to the earth. This in turn rests on one's Christology—the answer to the question "Who is the Lord Jesus Christ?" Virtually all Muslims of whom I am aware seem to admit that the New Testament contradicts Islam and argue that the New Testament has somehow been corrupted between the time of the first manuscripts and the life of Muhammed. To analyze this concept, consider one notorious case of a corrupted version of the Bible, the Wicked Bible of the 17th century. Through a printer's error, the Seventh Commandment read, "You shall commit adultery." Obviously the correct reading is "You shall not commit adultery." If there were one or two texts on which a controversy turns, the idea of a corrupted text might at least merit some thought. If many changes are required to harmonize two texts, then the idea of a corrupt text fades from logical view and we must face the fact that the New Testament and the Koran are fundamentally antagonistic from the start.

There are two related doctrines on which we can measure the theoretical possibility of corruption of the New Testament message: (1) Is Jesus Christ truly God or not? and (2) Will He return to earth as an ally of the Islamic Mahdi or as the Messiah-King in His own right? Most Islamic teachers claim that Jesus Christ will deny that He is God when He returns and that He will help the Mahdi establish Islamic rule over the earth. Some Islamic scholars believe that Jesus will undergo death after he has returned to the earth, in direct contradiction to Romans 6:8-9.

To start with the first question, we have to deal with alternative propositions: either Jesus Christ was misinterpreted when Christians taught that He is God, or He deceived His own disciples by claiming to be God if in fact this is false. So we can start by considering from the Holy Scriptures whether or not the Lord Jesus claimed to be God Almighty.

John in his writings especially stresses that Jesus was in fact God in human flesh. John 1:1, speaking of Jesus Christ, states simply that *"In the beginning was the Word, and the Word was with God and the Word was God. The same was in the beginning with God."* Then John 1:2 continues, *"All things were made by Him, and without Him was not anything made that was made."* Along with Colossians 1:15-16, John is ascribing to Jesus as He existed before His days in human flesh an integral part of the Creation. This accords with Genesis 1:26: *"Let Us make man in Our image, after Our likeness."* Already we can see that multiple and wide-ranging changes will be necessary to try to reconcile the Bible and the Koran.

The theme that Jesus Christ is the Son of God and in fact God in human flesh continues throughout the Gospel of John. John 1:14 refers to Jesus as "the only begotten of the Father." This dovetails with Luke's account of Jesus' birth in Luke 1:35, in which the good doctor explains that the Holy Spirit came upon Mary and the power of God impregnated her. In modern medical terms, the Holy Spirit planted a pure, holy sperm that fertilized one of Mary's ova so that Jesus was conceived fully God and fully man, perfect and without sin. Jesus' will was identical to His Father's will, but He could and did feel all the weaknesses of the human body such as pain and weariness and could experience temptation from outside His body and soul. This teaching is so different from the Muslim view that Jesus was merely a prophet that the two views cannot be mixed.

John the Baptist testified in John 1:30 that the Son of God long pre-existed him. Our Lord Jesus made the same claim in John 8:58: *"Before Abraham was, I AM."* The Pharisees were correct in observing that Jesus was not yet 50 years old (John 8:57) so far as His human body was concerned. So how could Jesus have seen Abraham? Because He was alive then, although not with the human body in which He came to earth. In fact, a careful reading of Genesis 18 (especially 18:21-22) indicates that the Lord Who descended to earth to inspect Sodom and its surroundings was in fact the Son of God, the same Person Who later came down in a human body. In this case He descended in a body that appeared human so that Abraham would not know the difference at first glance. But Abraham "stood before the Lord," which must mean the Son rather than the Father in context.

John 5 is especially explicit concerning the full equality between Father and Son. While on earth, as an example Jesus was subject to His Father and indeed as a child subject to His earthly mother and legal father as an example of a perfect child to all. Luke 2:51. As Paul wrote in Philippians 2:5, He *"did not think that equality with God was something to be clung to, but made Himself of no reputation . . ."* The Son had been equal to the Father but voluntarily subordinated Himself as part of His mission to *"save His people from their sins."* (Matthew 1:21) This eventually led to His shameful death on the Cross. Before then, our Lord Jesus taught plainly that He bears all of the authority of the Father with respect to the Judgment. *"For as the Father raises up the dead, and quickens, even so the Son quickens whom He wills. For the Father judges no man, but has committed all judgment to the Son, so that all men will honor the Son just as they honor the Father. He who does not honor the Son dishonors the Father Who sent Him."* John 5:21-23. (I have altered the translation slightly after consulting Strong's Concordance.

One might be more literal with the last sentence this way: *He who does not honor the Son absolutely does not honor the Father.*)

In historical terms I am defending the views concerning Jesus Christ of the church councils after Christianity became legal within the Roman Empire, such as the Council of Nicaea. I am defending Athanasius against Arius. On this question Augustine was right. Although there may be variations, Islam's view of Jesus Christ is a spin-off of heretical ideas debated and rejected by the early Christian Church. Mohammed did not go so far as to accept the view of the Sanhedrin that Jesus Christ was a heretic and a blasphemer who deserved to die. He did consider the Lord Jesus to be a great prophet and truly a human being. But Mohammed still balked at considering Jesus Christ as God in human flesh. His view fails the fundamental test of 1 John 2:21-23: *". . . [N]o lie is of the truth. Who is a liar but he that denies that Jesus is the Christ? He is antichrist who denies the Father and the Son. He who denies the Son has not the Father. He that acknowledges the Son has the Father also."* Mohammed's view denies the Sonship (see for example 1 John 1:3) and Kingship of Jesus Christ and in practical terms denies His Messiahship also, although Mohammed does accord the bare title of Messiah to Jesus. Psalms 2, 24, 45, 68 and 89 and the entire Book of Hebrews tell us much about the full meaning of Jesus as Messiah-King. Since Mohammed rejected these truths, as a Christian I can agree that Mohammed was am important historical figure whose movement displaced remaining idolatry in the Near East and in Iran. Much of the best of Greek knowledge was preserved under Islamic governments when this knowledge had been forgotten in Western Europe during the Dark Ages after the collapse of the Western Roman Empire. But I cannot embrace Mohammed as a true prophet of the living God because he did not worship the Lord Jesus Christ as God.

One view of true salvation in Jesus Christ as taught by the Bible involves the believer's acknowledgment, obedience and worship of Him. A subject of a human king will acknowledge the king's authority and obey that king. There is even a restricted form of deference in the form of physical gestures such as kneeling or bowing; all of these are limited by the king's fallibility and mortality. When a judge enters his or her courtroom, we stand out of respect for the judge's office and limited authority. The language we use conveys special respect.

We have already discussed acknowledgment, which involves principally the mind. Other passages will address this again. The Lord Jesus mentions obedience directly in Matthew 7. *"Not everyone who says to Me 'Lord, Lord' will enter the kingdom of heaven, but he who does the will of My Father Who is in heaven."* Matthew 7:21. *"Whoever hears these sayings of Mine and does them, I will liken him to a wise man who builds his house upon a rock"* Matthew 7:24, And again He said, *"Whosoever hears these sayings of Mine and does not do them shall be like a foolish man who builds his house on sand."* Matthew 7:26 The emphasis here is on obedience to the words of Jesus Christ as if they were the words of God, which indeed they were and still are. Hebrews 5:9 confirms this emphasis: *"He became the author of eternal salvation to all them who obey Him."* Acknowledgment is absolutely necessary, but by itself it is not good evidence of genuine conversion. As James said, *"The demons also believe and tremble."* James 2:19.

In addition to acknowledgment and obedience, worship is a necessary result of genuine salvation. In most of his epistles, the Apostle Paul called himself a slave of Jesus Christ. Paul and Barnabas refused worship of themselves when offered when they had performed healing miracles. Acts 14:13-18. In the gospels we see instances of real worship, including some that appear shocking to modern society. For example, the Apostle Thomas saw the evidence of His bodily resurrection and said to Jesus, *"My Lord and my God."* John 20:28. A more demonstrative instance is found in Luke 7:36-50, where the woman of a very questionable past nevertheless gave an illustration of true, all-out worship. In Matthew 26:6-13, Mark 14:3-9 and in John 12:1-8, we see other accounts of similar instances shortly before Jesus' crucifixion. Certainly with Jesus Christ now in heaven we cannot show the same physical demonstration of worship as these people, but their physical actions showed their inner commitment to Him. Nothing was held back. In principle our commitment to Jesus Christ needs to have that same unlimited quality. The full analogy between a marriage between one man and one woman and the relationship between Jesus Christ and each believer (and also between Jesus Christ and His Bride, the Church, as a whole) is a subject for another entire book. For present purposes, there is a full intimacy and a full commitment present even at initial conversion only partly understood that will take eternity to live out in full. For present purposes the point is that Mohammed's doctrine of Jesus Christ has no room for this relationship, and indeed Islam demands obedience to its understanding of God's commands without intimacy with God Himself or love between God and human beings. This falls short of the wonderful, loving provision that God has made through His Son Jesus Christ. So Islamic and Christian teachings are incompatible at this vital point.

QUESTION FOR REFLECTION & DISCUSSION:

Suppose you had been a dinner guest with Jesus Christ at Simon's house as recorded in Luke 7:36-50. How would you have reacted? What if someone of terrible reputation were to break down sobbing and screaming for mercy from God at your church during the sermon, like the publican in Luke 18:10-14?

Nobody is likely to try to sacrifice to us today, but how many people will try to flatter us instead? To what sins within us does flattery appeal? What are our spiritual defenses against flattery?

Returning to our quick survey of John's gospel for instances where Jesus Christ proclaimed Himself as God, in John 6:51 Jesus said, *"I am the living bread that came down from heaven."* Was Jesus really saying that He came from heaven instead of from earth? Yes, and only partially because of the Virgin Birth. He continued, *"Does this offend you? And what if you see the Son of Man ascend where He was before?"* John 6:61-62. Our Lord Jesus repeated his claim of heavenly origin in

John 7:28-29. In the figure of the manna, familiar to Jesus' hearers from the Exodus, and the wanderings in the Wilderness, Jesus throughout most of John 6 was claiming the power to grant eternal life, a power held only by God Himself. This claim and His related claims to be the Son of God and also the Son of Man are unique to Christianity and cannot be blended with any other faith. This is especially true when the Lord Jesus claimed to be the exclusive way to His Father: *"I am the Way, the Truth and the Life. No man comes to the Father except through Me."* John 14:6.

In John 8:46 Jesus Christ threw down the gauntlet: *"Which of you convicts Me of sin? And if I say the truth, why do you not believe Me?"* No mere man can dare challenge his contemporaries in that way. As Josh McDowell and C.S. Lewis often have pointed out, there is no middle ground to take as Mohammed and so many others of many persuasions attempt. The Lord Jesus was either God in human flesh as He claimed or a megalomaniac and a deceiver. So there can be no possible mistake of His claim, the Lord Jesus concluded, *"Before Abraham was, I AM."* (John 8:58) The Lord Jesus was claiming to have pre-existed Abraham. By using God's self-identification to Moses at the burning bush He claimed to be the same One who appeared to Moses. The Apostle Paul amplified this in 1 Corinthians 10, especially 10:4. Jesus' hearers made no mistake in understanding His claim. They tried to stone Him on the spot (John 8:59).

In John 10:30 the Lord Jesus stated flatly that *"I and My Father are one."* Once again John 10:33 makes it clear that the Jews listening to Jesus understood Him to claim to be God. Jesus made no effort either in John 8 or John 10 to tell his hearers that they had misunderstood. In fact they had understood quite well the substance of the claim, which most (although not Nicodemus as recorded in John 3:2) rejected in the face of Jesus' miracles and His teaching. So in substance Mohammed rejected the entire Gospel of John. It is not a question of stray corruption of a few isolated texts.

We should consider the last cleansing of the Temple recorded in Matthew 21:13, Mark 11:17 and in Luke 19:46. In all three of these Gospels our Lord Jesus called the Temple *"My house."* I have gone past this phrase without close attention until now. When our Lord Jesus referred earlier to the Temple in John 2:16, He called it *"My Father's house."* It was premature for the Lord Jesus to openly identify Himself as God and Messiah. At the end of His ministry when His time to be sacrificed was near, Jesus Christ asserted full ownership of the Temple in calling it *"My house."* Of course we know that the Temple has always been God's house since its dedication by Solomon and the reconstruction after the Exile in the time of Haggai. As the Lord Jesus spoke the Shekinah Glory was still behind the thick curtain, often called the veil because of its purpose even though it was anything but delicate as a bridal veil would be. This is still another claim among many of full equality with God on the part of Jesus Christ. At the same time the Temple was God's house and Jesus' house. As a co-owner of the Temple with God Jesus Christ was of the same substance as His Father and equally righteous with Him (consider Philippians 2:5-11 for the present reality and Matthew 25:31-46 and the entire book of Revelation for the future eternal reality), although temporarily housed in a human body and working and then suffering as a Servant to redeem us from our sin.

While the Gospel of Mark does not contain as great an emphasis as does the Gospel of John concerning Jesus Christ as God, the implications are there. For example, consider Mark 2:28, where Jesus said that *"the Son of Man is Lord also of the Sabbath."* Consider the implication here. The Sabbath is the fourth of the Ten Commandments given directly by God's voice. It was written on the Tablets that God have to Moses. Who would have the authority to alter the Fourth Commandment? A mere rabbi? Of course not. Only God can amend a commandment He has given; otherwise humanity has been given the authority to amend the Law of God. Even in human law, since when can an inferior authority change the law made by a superior authority, such as a State Legislature contradicting a valid law of Congress? Yet Jesus claimed the authority to define and even override the Sabbath. So the conclusion must be drawn that Jesus was claiming to be God and to bear God's authority in claiming the right to change the Sabbath law as given by His Father.

In Mark 16:19 we read that Jesus ascended into heaven after He rose from the dead. Can we as mortal human beings so ascend? Obviously not! And yet Jesus did. More than that, He sat down in the presence of God Almighty at His right hand. Being able to sit down at God's Table implies a special equality with God the Father that we do not have. The entire scene shows intimacy between Father and Son. A more detailed account of the Ascension is found in Acts 1.

A further point is raised in Mark 16:19: how can the Father be a father without a son? Permit me a personal example. I was born a child, and I gradually grew until I reached my full height and became an adult. While I was still single and even for a few years after I was married, I still was not a father. I became a father when my first child, a son, was conceived and then born. Likewise the Father in heaven cannot be a father without a son. Matthew 11:25-27 is another passage that stresses the relationship between the Father and His Son Jesus Christ. Even the familiar beginning of the Lord's Prayer, *"Our Father,"* implies the Father-Son relationship between God and Jesus Christ and also the Father-child relationship with each believer spelled out in more detail in Romans 8:14-17.

One of the points of emphasis in Matthew's gospel is the personal worship of the Son of God. A leper worshiped Jesus Christ in Matthew 8:2. His disciples worshiped Him in Matthew 14:33. The mother of the demon-possessed child worshiped Him in Matthew 15:25. The father of an insane child kneeled to Him in Matthew 17:14. When the Apostle Paul and Barnabas were offered worship, they were horrified and restrained the people (Acts 14:11-18). But Jesus Christ received the worship because it was right for people to worship Him because He was—and remains—God in human flesh, now a resurrected human body.

Many of the passages we have mentioned in Matthew and Mark have their counterparts in Luke. There is another passage (Luke 19:30-35) that points to the deity of Jesus Christ, dealing with the colt on which He rode into Jerusalem. When the disciples were accosted by the owners as the disciples were untying the colt to take it to Jesus Christ, as instructed by Him the disciples told the owners that *"the Lord has need of him (the colt)."* Luke 19:31,34. As Psalm 24:1 says, *"The earth is the Lord's and the fulness of it; the world and they that dwell in it."* Job expressed the general principle at the start of his suffering: *"The Lord gave and the Lord has taken away; blessed be the name of the Lord."* Job 1:21. What the Lord Jesus was doing was asserting his paramount rights of ownership over that colt as a tiny piece of the fulness of the earth. The human property rights of the owners had to give way to the divine right of God on earth. The owners wisely accepted the explanation and let the colt go without further challenge or explanation. Here again the Lord Jesus performed an act reserved to God.

There are several passages such as Matthew 17:9-12 and Matthew 20:18-19 in which the Lord predicts His suffering and death. All of these as well as Psalm 22 and 69 contradict the notion that someone other than Jesus Christ died on the Cross. In my previous book *Fighting the Good Fight* (published by Trafford Publishing Company, 2011, at pp. 311-312), I through a fictional prisoner described how a person would reason that it was Jesus and not Judas or someone else on the Cross based on the seven last words spoken by Jesus Christ on the Cross. To take one example, Judas would not have arranged for the future care of Jesus' mother. Nor would Judas have guaranteed paradise to another inmate, as Jesus did. Finally, Judas was already dead by suicide before Jesus was nailed to the Cross (Matthew 27:3-5). Judas therefore could not have been on the Cross.

Jesus Christ also predicted that He would rise from the dead, which of necessity predicts His death first. Matthew 16:21, 17:23, 20:19; Mark 9:31, 10:34; Luke 9:22, 18:33, 24:6-7. Even His enemies were aware of His claim that He would rise from the dead. Matthew 27:62-66. Jesus never backed away from His claim that He would rise from the dead. Consider also the accounts of the darkened sky at noon and the earthquake at the hour of Jesus' death. The graves of many were opened and the veil in the Temple was torn from top to bottom, in symbol showing that the way to the Mercy Seat was now open (Matthew 27:51-53). All of these unusual phenomena in the physical world were part of God's witness to His acceptance of His Son's sacrifice for sin and His resurrection from the dead. There is also the fact that resurrected servants of God appeared to people in Jerusalem after Jesus Christ rose from the dead.

The idea that God and Jesus cooperated to fake the death of Jesus Christ on the Cross (and also the variant claim of books such as <u>Passover Plot</u> that Jesus intended to stage both His death and His resurrection) is an attack on the truthfulness of both the Father and the Son. We have already discussed and discarded the idea that Judas or someone else was on the Cross. It was Jesus the Messiah-King Who was crucified and killed. Of His death there can be no realistic doubt, because it was certified by professional executioners experienced in their grim occupation.

Mohammed concedes that Jesus rose to heaven at some point shortly after His trial, so Mohammed is implicitly conceding that Jesus was approved by God. We know that God excludes liars from heaven (Revelation 21:8). If Jesus Christ had been lying about His death and resurrection, then how could a totally holy God (Isaiah 6:1-7, for example) receive Jesus into heaven? In fact the Lord Jesus was the living Truth and the Son of God, so His total and complete access to His Father was simply a restoration of the normal access He had had before time began.

Jesus Christ approved as truth an answer by a lawyer which distilled the entire Old Testament into two commandments:

You shall love the Lord your God with all your heart, all your soul, all your strength and all your mind; and your neighbor as yourself. Luke 10:27. Yet Islam says practically nothing of this form of sacrificial love (Greek *agape*). This leads to profound differences in manner of life and ethics, which are too broad to summarize here. To take but one illustration, Islam permits polygamy where Christianity forbids it (see especially 1 Corinthians 7:1-5 and Matthew 19:1-10).

While there is much more to this topic, this is enough to make the point that Mohammed in practice rejected the central themes of the New Testament concerning Jesus Christ. There is no issue of a corrupted text, but rather an irrepressible conflict (in the phrase of William Seward concerning freedom against slavery) between the teachings of Mohammed and the teachings of Jesus Christ.

QUESTIONS FOR REFLECTION AND DISCUSSION:

1. Do we respect the Lord Jesus as a great teacher and essentially stop there or do we also worship Him as Almighty God?
2. How strongly do we believe that He died and rose from the dead as historical facts? (Read 1 Corinthians 15 for the supreme importance of this issue.) What does His resurrection mean for us?

In summary, I would affirm that Jesus Christ will return in triumph and victory to the earth as Messiah-King and will reign forever and ever. We will share His eternal life. For now let us bypass the subsidiary issue of whether there will be a 1000-year Millenium on this earth before the new heavens and new earth come into being. Our Lord Jesus will bear allegiance to His Father as He always has, but He will be subordinate to no one else. We will all be at His service forever. *"Now to the King eternal, immortal, invisible, the only wise God, [be] honor and glory forever and ever. Amen!* 1 Timothy 1:17. And again, *"Unto Him Who loved us and washed us from our sins in His own blood, and has made us kings and priests to God and His Father, to Him [be] glory and dominion forever and ever. Amen! Behold, He comes with clouds and every eye shall see Him, and they that pierced Him, and all kindreds of the earth shall wail because of Him. Even so, Amen!* Revelation 1:5-7

QUESTION FOR REFLECTION AND DISCUSSION:

When Jesus Christ returns, will you wail or rejoice? On what do you base your answer?

APPENDIX B —
A NOTE ON GLORY

In 1 Corinthians 2:8, the Holy Spirit through the Apostle Paul called Jesus Christ "the Lord of Glory." In line with this, Paul wrote, *"God forbid that I should glory except in the Cross of Jesus Christ my Lord . . ."* Galatians 6:14. So humanity has no glory of its own, as is also taught in Isaiah 40:6-8: *"All flesh is grass and the goodliness of it as the flower of the field. The grass withers; the flower fades because the Spirit of the Lord blows on it. Surely the people is grass. The grass withers; the flower fades, but the word of our God shall stand forever."* This is quoted in 1 Peter 1:24-25. The very fact that the Lord Jesus has glory whereas human beings of themselves have none is still another proof that He is God.

Matthew 25:31 introduces the subject of the Last Judgment by saying, *"When the Son of Man comes in His glory, and all the holy angels with Him, then shall He sit on the throne of His glory."* This is another verse that I have been prone to read over quickly. But what does His glory really mean? I do not expect to comprehend all of it while I remain in this temporary tabernacle before I depart this earth, but that is no excuse to ignore the subject. When I consult Strong's Concordance, I see that the word "glory" is translated from the Greek *doxa*, which is the same root from which we derive the words Doxology and orthodox. Since I know that the Doxology is a musical setting of Psalm 100, one aspect of the glory of God can be studied there. I will leave the details for you, but Psalm 100 starts with praise to God. So one start toward glorifying God is praise in which the whole heart, soul, mind and strength is engaged. The word orthodox is a compound of two Greek roots: <u>ortho</u> means "right" and the other is *"doxa,"* translated glory. So orthodoxy literally means giving God the glory that is rightfully His. This usually is considered in terms of correct doctrine, which is vital. But I think that more than doctrine is involved here. To be fully orthodox in its broad sense would mean to fulfill Luke 10:27. Once again, we will never meet this standard while we are in this body, but that is no excuse not to start.

When I consult <u>Strong's Concordance</u>, I see mention of dignity, glory, honor, praise and worship. All of these things apply to Jesus Christ, the Lord of Glory. One certainly can see dignity in Psalms 24 and 45, both of which portray the Messiah Jesus as King. Psalm 2 and practically the entire Book of Hebrews relate to His authority. So does much of the Gospel of Matthew, especially from Matthew 19 to the end of the book. As to His glory, the passages of the Transfiguration (Matthew 17:1-13; Mark 9:1-13; Luke 9:28-36) and Revelation 1 are a visual portrait. Consider also 2 Thessalonians 2:8, which tells us that the Wicked shall be destroyed by the Lord Jesus *"with the brightness of His coming."* We know that we cannot look directly at the Sun lest we become blind. Similarly, John, the most intimate of the Apostles with Jesus Christ, nevertheless fell down as if dead when he saw Him in His resurrected state. Revelation 1:17.

As to praise and worship of Jesus Christ, I cannot now venture deeply into subjects that would justify at least one entire book each. The entire Book of Psalms would be one place to start. For those who are visually minded, Isaiah 6 and Revelation 5, 8, 14 and 19-22 might be one way to start despite the mystery of some things. Thomas' confession of John 20:28 is succinct and simple in its basics, although its full implications are vast. I come back to three elements of true salvation and conversion being acknowledgment, obedience and worship. One reason that Jesus Christ has the right to all this is because of His glory.

APPENDIX C —
CELEBRATIONS GOOD AND BAD IN SCRIPTURE

Given the disastrous end of Belshazzar's party as recorded in Daniel 6, one is tempted to avoid all parties as evil. It is true that many modern parties today lead to tragedies. But the view of the Scriptures is not that rigid, although it is full of warnings about the consequences of drunkenness. For example Proverbs 23:29-35 warns that strong drink in quantity is like a snake:

Who has woe? Who hath sorrow? Who has arguments? Who has babbling? Who has wounds without cause? Who has redness of eyes?

They that tarry long at the wine; they that go to seek mixed wine.

Look not thou upon the wine when it is red, when it giveth his color in the cup; it moves itself aright.

At the last it bites like a serpent and stings like an adder.

Your eyes shall behold strange women, and your heart shall utter perverse things.

Yes, you shalt be as he that lies down in the midst of the sea, or as he that lies upon the top of a mast.

They have stricken me. I was not sick; they have beaten me, I did not feel it: when shall I awake? I will seek it yet again.

Proverbs 23:1-3 also warns of the perils of overeating and of dinner parties in general:

When you sit down to eat with a ruler, consider diligently what [is] before you. Put a knife to your throat if you are a man given to appetite. Do not desire his dainties, for they are deceitful food.

Solomon of all people as a wealthy king knew of the perils of royal social life. On Wall Street and in Washington and around the world, people are often invited to parties to be set up to deliver favors later. True friendship is rarely involved. Solomon's warnings are as pertinent today as they were then. But the Scriptures also teach that there are right times to celebrate. We will attempt to take each Biblical instance of a party for what it says.

The Scriptures are not clear as to whether Noah and his family were having a family celebration when he became drunk in Genesis 9:21. It is not totally clear whether Noah even realized that he could be intoxicated from the wine, since grapes may have been new to him. It is also possible to believe that Noah and his family were celebrating their survival of the Flood and their first crops and that Noah got carried away. Either way, there were long-term consequences because Ham looked at his father in his naked state, dishonoring his human father. The consequences did not fall on Ham but on the descendants of Canaan, one of Ham's children (Genesis 10:6). Centuries later, the Canaanites were ousted from what was then the Promised Land by the children of Israel under the command of Joshua, with consequences that remain to this day. This invasion and conquest fulfilled God's curse upon Canaan and his promise to Abraham so far as earthly territory is concerned. The children of Abraham (Ishmael and Isaac, leading to the modern-day Arabs and Jews) have displaced the descendants of

Ham from Egypt and the Holy Land, with results that make headlines virtually every week.

Centuries after Noah's drunkenness, Abraham also had a party to celebrate the weaning of Isaac, his son of promise with his wife Sarah, as recorded in Genesis 21:8-10. At the party, Ishmael, the older son from Sarah's servant Hagar, mocked Isaac instead of loving him like a brother. As a result, Hagar and Ishmael were forced to leave permanently. God provided for them; Hagar herself was a woman of faith. But there was a lasting separation between the descendants of Isaac and the descendants of Ishmael. This has proved true and endured both territorially and spiritually. Both of these divisions were in the plan of God, but we should also learn how a seemingly small incident can have enduring consequences.

Roughly two centuries later, Pharaoh had a party on his birthday (Genesis 40:20). Joseph was confined in prison as the head trusty. Pharaoh's butler and baker were held there on suspicion of attempting to poison Pharaoh. Each of them had a dream, and Joseph understood correctly that the butler would be restored to his position and that the baker would be executed. While only God knows for sure, the butler was probably innocent because apparently Pharaoh was not in further danger upon the butler's release. Likewise it is probable that the baker was guilty because the Bible makes no mention of God's displeasure at his execution. But two years later, the effects of this party and of the aides' dreams was to make itself apparent with the release and elevation of Joseph to the second position in all of Egypt. Joseph's stewardship put Egypt on the way to become an ancient Great Power and ensured the survival of Israel in the providence of God. Once more great consequences came from a party that seemed insignificant.

After the Exodus, the Israelites held a party while Moses was communing with God on the mountain. (Exodus 32) With Moses gone, the people of Israel panicked because as a whole they had no faith of their own. So they gave their gold to Aaron, who made the Golden Calf. They also threw a party, which Moses and Joshua heard coming down the mountain. The first result is that the people lost most of their gold, because the Golden Calf was ground to pieces and thrown into water. Moses made the people drink from it (Exodus 32:20). So the gold was eventually eliminated in their bodily wastes—a fit ending for an idol. Worse, about 3000 people died that day because of the idolatry (Exodus 32:28). The faithlessness that caused this party to be thrown kept recurring, which eventually resulted in the entire Exodus generation from 20 years of age and higher to die in the Wilderness without ever reaching the Promised Land.

We have already discussed Daniel 6, Belshazzar's awful party. We cannot say how many of the guests were killed that night, but we know that Belshazzar died for his impiety and that Daniel survived and even thrived. Blessed Daniel was for not having been originally invited! It took the handwriting on the wall to make anyone willing to listen to Daniel and receive the sentence of judgment from God. This particular party was the final straw that triggered regime change and the rise of Persia.

Coming forward a few decades from Daniel to Esther, we have one party thrown by Haman and two consecutive dinner parties hosted by Queen Esther (see Esther 5-7 for more detail). Haman threw his party as a preliminary to his coming campaign to exterminate the Jews (Esther 5:10-14). There followed the construction of a gallows. Queen Esther threw her two dinner parties to confront Haman and to arrest the progress of his plot to kill all the Jews. God intervened by providence to cause the King to learn of Mordecai's loyalty (Mordecai was a leading Jew at the time, with Daniel having died) while these parties were been planned and given. The ultimate consequence was that the King was shocked at the enormity of Haman's scheme. When Haman tried to beg Queen Esther for his life, the King interpreted that as an attempt to rape Esther and ordered Haman hanged from his own gallows. He then allowed the Jews to defend themselves from Haman's now headless putsch. The consequence was the survival of the Jews both in former Babylonian lands and in Israel itself through the periods of Persian and Greek rule. There was a Jewish population to hear Jesus Christ during His ministry on earth.

So far, some negative and even tragic consequences have followed from every party we have examined. One could add the birthday party that resulted in the beheading of John the Baptist. Does this mean that we are never to celebrate? No! God commanded feasts as part of the religious life of Israel, as a study of the seven major Jewish holidays would show. Solomon's feast at the dedication of the First Temple was a wonderful time (1 Kings 8). In fact, Michal's inability to celebrate with King David when the Tabernacle came home was the final blow to their marriage (2 Samuel 6:20-23). Our Lord Jesus attended a wedding and even made wine miraculously from water when the wine ran short. (John 2:1-11) One criticism of Jesus during His human life was that His disciples did not fast regularly as other Jews did. (Matthew 9:14-17; Mark 2:18-22). Perhaps He and His disciples were too joyful for others' taste. We need to be careful how we celebrate and why we celebrate, but believers in Jesus Christ with the sure promise from God of eternal life have every reason to celebrate in joy and sobriety.

There is one everlasting party yet to come which we must not miss. This is the marriage supper of Jesus Christ, the Lamb of God and Bridegroom. It is described briefly in Revelation 21:1-4. In Matthew 26:29, Mark 14:25 and in Luke 22:18 the Lord Jesus told His disciples that He would not drink the fruit of the vine again after the Last Supper until He would drink it again with them in His Father's kingdom. This should be part of that great marriage supper.

In parables our Lord Jesus on at least two occasions uses the marriage supper as an illustration of salvation and entrance into His kingdom. One of these is the parable of the 10 virgins in Matthew 25:1-13. In that parable being a virgin—by analogy, outward keeping of the Law—was not enough. One needed the oil of the Holy Spirit within to enter. Another is found in Matthew 22:1-14, again dealing with a marriage supper. In this case the King sent invitations to the expected guests, but they were too busy to come. Even though the pursuits of the invited guests were legitimate enough, that was no excuse for declining the invitation. There can be nothing more important than an invitation from the King—particularly from Jesus Christ, the King of all Creation and Prince of Peace. Disregarding the invitation was an insult to the King. Disregarding God's invitation to be saved from sin by His grace through the sacrifice of His Son Jesus Christ is an infinitely graver slight than (to take a recent example) declining an invitation from the White House.

The guest who entered without a wedding garment was like a modern party-crasher. In ancient times the bridegroom supplied the wedding garment. The party-crasher wanted to come on his own terms, like someone who wants to come to Christ without changing his conduct. If the oil represents the Spirit within, the wedding garment represents the outward changes caused by the Spirit's entrance. If we seek Jesus Christ, we must seek Him on His terms. We cannot negotiate a peace treaty with Him as if we are an independent sovereign. He rightfully demands unconditional surrender. If we are even prudent or wise, we will surrender immediately to enter His kingdom by His grace through faith in Him and in Him alone.

A FINAL WORD

People of many faiths are given different prescriptions of how to reach heaven. Certainly medieval Catholicism, Islam, Buddhism and various other religions differ widely from one another, but all of them start with one common question that some Jewish people asked the Lord Jesus when He walked the earth: *"What shall we do, that we might work the works of God?"* John 6:28. The Philippian jailer, shaken to his core by an earthquake, asked Paul and Silas a very similar question: *"What must I do to be saved?"* Acts 16:30. Both of these questions have in common the concept that we are capable of doing something to enter the salvation and kingdom of God, if we could only find out the formula, like the combination of a safe. In fact this entire concept is wrong. Our Lord Jesus answered in John 6:29, *"This is the work of God, that you believe on Him Whom He has sent."* Paul's and Silas' answer in Acts 16:31 was likewise simple: *Believe on the Lord Jesus Christ and you will be saved, and your house."* The common element in the answers is <u>faith.</u> Faith, not works, is the portal to the kingdom of God. *"For by grace are you saved through faith, and that not of yourselves. It is the gift of God, not of works, lest any man should boast."* Ephesians 2:8-9. Ephesians 2:10 and the entire book of James make it very clear that good works will follow faith and be the evidence of faith to the world, but works good in the sight of God always come after faith, not before.

The Biblical idea of salvation as the free gift of God (Romans 6:23—note that death is earned as wages but that eternal life is given) cannot be mixed with an earned salvation of any variety. Salvation is not even partially earned. Romans 4:1-11 and 11:6 are especially strong in maintaining that our own works have nothing to do with our salvation from sin. This dovetails with Colossians 1:13, where Paul through the Holy Spirit write that we have been *"delivered us from the kingdom of darkness and has translated us to the kingdom of His dear Son."* We are not brought to a point where we have a chance to attain the kingdom, but we are brought all the way into the kingdom. The mercy and grace of God are complete through the saving work of Jesus Christ.

The various figures used to portray the unsaved person before conversion all show that person's helplessness and dependence on divine mercy. A leper could never heal himself or herself. Naaman the Syrian, a general and a leper, was just as helpless in himself as a poor person. His story is found in 2 Kings 5. He would have done some great feat for his healing and came prepared to pay. But the healing was free and no great feat was asked. Symbolically in washing in the Jordan, Naaman was admitting his sin and helplessness and also the supremacy of the God of Israel and placing his faith in Him. The seven times symbolized completeness, just as in our culture seven games is a complete World Series. A person *"dead in trespasses and sins"* (Ephesians 2:1) was utterly unable to resurrect himself or herself. A wild branch cannot graft himself or herself into the olive tree (Romans 11:17). We can do nothing whatsoever to earn salvation or even to make ourselves inherently attractive to God. We may be rich or poor, healthy or sick, respected or despised. In whatever condition we are in, we must ask to be saved as at Peter's first sermon. *"Men, brethren, what shall we do?"* Peter responded, *"Repent and be baptized every one of you in the name of Jesus Christ for the remission of sins, and you will be given the gift of the Holy Spirit."* (Acts 2:37-38)

No conversion is immediately total or perfect. But common elements are (1) Admission of one's sin and an honest desire to turn away from it; (2) Intellectual and emotional embracing that Jesus Christ is fully God and Man, and that He and He alone has paid the death penalty for our sin, rose from the dead and can now set us free; and (3) An honest commitment to live for Him—after all, He died for us. You cannot do this yourself any more than a baby could by his or her own efforts leave the womb (see John 3:1-21). So you must ask Him to do it for you and to you. I plead with you to take time to do that now. *"Behold, now is the accepted time. Now is the day of salvation."* 2 Corinthians 6:2.